WESTMOUNT SCHOOL
120 W. Begin Street
THUNDER BAY, ONTARIO
P7E 5M4

This copy of **"Performance"**
was donated
to your library courtesy of
**The Thunder Bay
Historical Museum Society**

PERFORMANCE

BY GEORGE CAMPBELL

Link Publishing Co., a division of Link Inc.

To the performers...
past, present and future.

Yours is the gift and ours the reward.
Thank you for enriching our lives.

0-1 Artist's rendering of the Thunder Bay Community Auditorium

0-2 Clan MacGillivray Pipe Band, Port Arthur, Ontario, July 12, 1920 T.B.Mus.

© 1985 Link Publishing Co., a division of Link Inc.

All rights reserved. No part of this publication may be reproduced, stored in a retrieval system, or transmitted in any form or by any means, electronic, mechanical, photocopying, recording, or otherwise, without the prior written permission of Link Publishing Co., 432 North Syndicate Avenue, Thunder Bay, Ontario, P7C 3W7.

Care has been taken to trace the ownership of the photos used in the text. The publisher welcomes any information that will enable him to correct any reference or credit in future editions.

ISBN 0-9692283-0-9

Published by Link Publishing Co., a division of Link Inc., 432 North Syndicate Avenue, Thunder Bay, Ontario, P7C 3W7.

CO-ORDINATING EDITOR: Gregory D. Cheadle
PHOTO RESEARCH: Janet Anderson
PHOTOGRAPHY: Vivid Photos
RESEARCH: Jo Kulick, George Campbell
DESIGN: Sherron McIvor
TYPESETTING: Guide Printing and Publishing
SEPARATIONS: Image Colour
LITHOGRAPHY: Lakehead Printing & Stenographic Services Limited
BINDING: Phil-Mar Trade Bindery Ltd.

PAPER: colour signatures, 100 lb. Jenson Gloss, Provincial Papers;
       black & white signatures, 186M Phoenix Imperial, Cover White Dull, Papierfabrik Scheufelen
TIPPING: 210M T2000 RO, Zanders Feinpapiere AG
END PAPER: 74 lb. Elephant Hide, Zanders Feinpapiere AG

The text for this book was set by Guide Printing and Publishing, Thunder Bay, Ontario. The body copy is set $10\frac{1}{2}/11\frac{1}{2}$ Souvenir, the heads in $10\frac{1}{2}/11\frac{1}{2}$ Souvenir Bold, the quotes in $11\frac{1}{2}/12\frac{1}{2}$ Souvenir Bold Italic and the captions in $8\frac{1}{2}/9$ Souvenir Italic.

Printed in Canada

Contents

DEDICATION iii
AUTHOR'S PREFACE vii
FOREWORD ix
THE GOVERNOR GENERAL xi
LETTER FROM THE PRIME MINISTER xiii
LETTER FROM THE PREMIER xv
CITY OF THUNDER BAY COAT OF ARMS xvi
MUNICIPALITIES xvii
TRIBUTE TO DR. CHARLES JOHNSTON xviii

Humble Beginnings 1
Leadership 17
Choirs 33
The Dance 49
Drama and Theatre 61
Bands and Musicians 97
Rock and Roll 109
The Orchestra 121
The Auditorium 137
The Opening 157

BOARD OF DIRECTORS 157
SPONSORSHIPS 158
PHOTO ACKNOWLEDGEMENTS 163
ABOUT THE AUTHOR 164

Thunder Bay Community Auditorium

AUTHOR'S PREFACE

To try writing a history of the performing arts in Thunder Bay, is really to risk crucifixion. The ones you please will applaud you, and the ones you insult will be deeply hurt. And unless you have years and years in which to do your research, you're bound to divide your readership into the two groups.

Let me therefore apologize to those who will feel that I ignored them. Believe me, it was not intentional. I tried very hard, under the circumstances peculiar to the project, to at least find out about everybody. Thus, I believe I did the best that was possible within the given parameters.

Of needs then, this is not a complete history. I would nevertheless hope that when you finish reading it, you'll appreciate the truly magnificent story of the performing arts in our city. To tell it completely, would require more than one book, for it is truly an epic.

We've had, and still have, some wonderful artists at the Lakehead, and most of them were/are amateurs. These people do their things strictly for the enjoyment of performing. You and I support them by buying their tickets, coming to their productions, and applauding them when they finish.

By all means, let us continue to do that -- and support our professionals, too -- and especially, let us not be afraid to *stand up* to applaud them, for these people often give us performances that are as good or better than similar efforts anywhere else in this country. That's because our people right here in Northwestern Ontario are just as good as anybody else in Canada. And I will qualify that no further.

In conclusion, I must thank a great many people for helping me gather the information that went into this. I thank those of you who were available when I needed information. Without your memories, I couldn't have done it at all. I also thank Mr. Greg Cheadle for making this project possible in the first place, and a special thanks to Mrs. Jo Kulik for her help in collecting the bits and pieces. Last, but not least, I must thank my good wife, Ruth, for continuing to live with me while the project was in progress.

George Campbell,
Kakabeka Falls, Ont.,
August, 1985.

0-3

0-4

0-5

0-3   B.G. Smalley with church choir and orchestra shortly after First World War   T.B.Mus.

0-4   Huck Heerema, one of the region's most popular entertainers in the 1970s

0-5   Fort William Girls' Band marching up Court Street past Fire Hall, July 1941   T.B.Mus.

FOREWORD

What an adventure in discovery. Uncovering such a wealth of talent and so many examples of selflessness through the years is nothing less than inspiring. These pages recount only some of the people, places, events and struggles to provide us all with other views of this voyage called life. Art in any of its forms provides sustenance for the soul as sport does for the body or education for the mind. Mankind knows no greater or more beneficial statement of its accomplishments than that revealed through its artistic expression. The desire of the entertainer to perform requires so much more commitment than an audience ever knows.

Inspiring too has been the eagerness of so many who assisted in this publishing project. The Thunder Bay Historical Museum Society pulled out all the stops for us and without their able assistance much would have been missed. The Brodie Resource Library and Lakehead University's Chancellor Norman M. Paterson Library all provided quick, competent help when it was requested. The various organizations and, in many cases, key individuals allowed us access to private collections and scrap books. Without them we simply could not have completed our research. The book team, members of the media, people from the auditorium, symphony, dance and theatre representatives and even admirers of the arts all came together to help ensure the accuracy and interest of the history represented here.

As is so often the case, there are people who help in areas indirectly connected with a project. To John Ranta, Ken Boshcoff and Larry Dustin, a most sincere thank-you. To the Board of Directors and administration of the Thunder Bay Community Auditorium Inc. go great thanks for without your seal of approval this book might not have happened.

The real people though, who truly brought this book into existence are George Campbell who researched and wrote the text in just thirty-nine days, Janet Anderson who over-saw the photo research and reproduction and Sherron McIvor, the designer whose talent put all the pieces together so beautifully. These are the three who did it.

Now we have our Auditorium! Finally, we will be able to enjoy entertainers both great and humble. Above all though, we must remember "The greatest artist was once a beginner".

Gregory D. Cheadle,
Publisher.

HER EXCELLENCY THE RIGHT HONOURABLE JEANNE SAUVE
GOVERNOR GENERAL OF CANADA

PRIME MINISTER · PREMIER MINISTRE

I am very pleased to offer my greetings and best wishes to the people of Thunder Bay on the occasion of the opening of your new Community Auditorium.

The completion of this Auditorium represents an exciting addition to the performing arts scene in Thunder Bay, one that will permit you to enjoy the best in quality entertainment. As well, the Auditorium promises to be an important focal point for rising young talents from Thunder Bay and Northwestern Ontario, and will provide them with the calibre of encouragement and support they need to succeed.

I am very proud that the Federal Government was able to assist in the development of this wonderful facility, and I wish to commend the citizens of Thunder Bay for all they have done to ensure its success.

OTTAWA
1985

xiii

Ontario

Parliament Buildings
Queen's Park
Toronto, Ontario
M7A 1A1

The Premier
of Ontario

October 16, 1985

On behalf of the people and the Government of Ontario, I am delighted to extend through the pages of this commemorative book my warmest best wishes on the occasion of the opening of the Thunder Bay Community Auditorium.

A performing arts centre that will bring theatrical and cultural presentations to the residents of Thunder Bay and all of Northwestern Ontario, the Thunder Bay Community Auditorium is a tribute to the commitment of the province and the community to the promotion of the arts. I have every confidence that it will be a valued addition to the City of Thunder Bay and that it will be a source of enjoyment and entertainment for young and old alike.

A great debt of gratitude is owed to all those who have made this auditorium possible. I am pleased that the Government of Ontario has been able to provide extensive support for this project and trust that it will serve the community well for many years to come.

May I convey my best wishes for the outstanding success of the Thunder Bay Community Auditorium.

David Peterson

xv

MUNICIPALITIES

District of Thunder Bay

Geraldton
Longlac
Beardmore
Manitouwadge
Marathon
Nipigon
Red Rock
Schreiber
Terrace Bay

District of Rainy River

Fort Frances
Atikokan

District of Kenora

Dryden
Ignace

TRIBUTE TO DR. CHARLES M. JOHNSTON

In the early summer of 1982 the Thunder Bay Community Auditorium was looking over a list of community names that might be considered to take over the job of President and Chairman of the Board of Directors of the organization. The next president to be recommended for appointment was going to be a critical decision. We had to find an outstanding community leader who shared the vision about the facility in order to provide firm leadership while dealing with a number of major hurdles which were still before us.

A name that came to mind immediately was that of Dr. Charles Johnston. He served with distinction as Chairman of the Board of Governors of Confederation College from 1968 to 1974 and was involved in the debate about where the college should be located. He always liked a good hard-fought battle here and there. Most importantly he had a deep concern and commitment to young people and the people of Northwestern Ontario.

Dr. Johnston had a very distinguished medical career, but is best known for his accomplishments in the community; such as:
- Alderman, City of Thunder Bay 1970-74. He was very involved in working for amalgamation of the two cities.
- Mayor of Athlete's Village, 1981 Canada Summer Games.
- President, Lakehead Chamber of Commerce.
- Past Chairman, Confederation College Board of Governors.
- Member of the Council of Regents, Ontario Colleges of Applied Arts and Technology.
- Past President, Ontario Heart Foundation, Thunder Bay Chapter.
- Past Chairman, Port Arthur Board of Education.
- Past President of Thunder Bay Medical Society.
- Past President, Gyro Club of Port Arthur.

He held various positions in the local medical field:
- Past President of the Port Arthur General Hospital Medical Staff.
- Served as Chief of Staff at the Port Arthur General Hospital.
- Past Chief of Obstetrics and Gynaecology at Port Arthur General and St. Joseph's Hospitals.

And in 1972, he was made Fellow of the Royal College of Physicians and Surgeons.

We were so fortunate to convince Dr. Johnston and his number one fan and supporter, his gracious wife Florence, to officially become involved in the Community Auditorium as a team.

As President he dug right in and commenced doing, as he had a firm belief in not just giving direction but in helping to get the jobs done. He tackled all the ensuing issues that we were to face with dignity, honesty, a great deal of decorum and in a business-like fashion.

He handled each issue straight on with an openness to new ideas but a strong conviction that once the pros and cons were discussed it was time to make a decision and press on. He would constantly seek out views and opinions from a wide spectrum of people and open a line of communication to find solutions when at times there appeared to be none.

After more than a decade of studies, debates, reviews, more studies, debates and reviews, the Auditorium with Dr. Johnston at the helm, successfully weathered a final trio of storms . .
- an Ontario Municipal Board Hearing.
- an Environmental Assessment Hearing, and,
- a municipal plebiscite

On June 18, 1985, Dr. Johnston died, less than four months before opening night.

As in other things he tackled in his life, he played a key leadership role in gathering support for the building of the facility. It is unfortunate that he could not be here for the official opening and to see the building being used by the community. But all of us who worked with him as part of the team know he will always be with us in spirit.

"I'm standing here before you
I don't know what I bring
If you can hear the music
Why don't you help me sing"
         Leonard Cohen

J.G. (Jim) Rapino

xx

1-1

Humble Beginnings

Humble Beginnings

1-1   Miss Sylvia Horn performs in "Gigohetto", a musical comedy performed at the Orpheum Theatre in a Grace Ensworth recital, 1925

... The performing arts are as old as language ...

... they also found time to sing, dance and create their legends ...

JUST AS THERE HAVE BEEN PEOPLE IN THIS AREA FOR A LONG, long time, so there has been music, song, story and dance, for such things go with people wherever they wander, and are handed down from generation to generation. Therefore, it is as impossible to say when such things first arrived here as it is to pinpoint the first human visitor, but we can be sure that when the one came, so did the other.

According to those who know, the last glaciers melted through here about 10,600 years ago. Local archeologists say that North American aborigines were using the Kaministikwia for at least 2,000 years before white men arrived, which extrapolates to at least 350 B.C. The point is that like every other ethnic group that followed them, those people settled here to make their living, and found the task difficult. Thus, to ease the drudgery of finding bare essentials, they also found time to sing, dance, and create their legends, and to this day, their Native Indian descendants share that heritage with all the rest of the ethnic collage that now calls itself Thunder Bay.

The same thing happened elsewhere. First came primitive peoples, and then very gradually, modern civilizations evolved. But always, wherever this has happened, there has also developed a marked affinity to perform and listen, to show and watch, and above all to participate. The performing arts, in other words, are uniquely human and as old as language. They've been a vital part of every race that has lived on this Earth.

The *Coureurs de bois* who came here with Radisson and Grosseilliers in the 1650s, with Daniel Greysolon, Sieur Du Lhut in 1679, with Zacherie de la Noue in 1717, and with La Verendre in 1731, undoubtedly brought a fiddle or a fife, if not some other instrument of the day. They found time during the long winters to rekindle their spirits with song or dance and ribald story. Their music came from old France, and had long since sunk into their heritage even then. Consequently, it came with them here to the Kaministikwia, and stayed long after they had gone.

In fact, we still sing and whistle those happy songs of theirs, even today, and so the next time you hear *Frere Jacques* or *Au Pres de ma Blonde*, reflect a moment on just how long such tunes have been heard right here in Thunder Bay. They're now part of our heritage, too.

The singing of traditional French songs continued after 1763, even though Scottish merchants took over the old French fur trade, and the Gentlemen Adventurers became Trading Partners, and the *coureurs de bois* became *voyageurs*. By then, the rousing old French songs had acquired distinctive new words, but were still sung at their best in Quebecois.

Voyageurs sang almost as long as they were awake, and they usually got little sleep. They often had to paddle 18 hours a day, portage, repair canoes, and do whatever else needed to be done, and they sang as they worked. While paddling, they sang to set their rhythmn - 40 strokes per minute, hour after hour. To a voyageur, singing was as natural as paddling, and he learned both at an early age. He heard singing and music at home all the time, and so he sang in the wilderness to ease the monotony of his terrible toil, just as sailors did before him, and cowboys and lumberjacks did after him.

Imagine yourself standing beside a mist shrouded lake on a dew soaked summer morning 175 years ago. Imagine a voyageur brigade coming towards you from far across the lake, completely hidden by the morning mist. The sound of their singing would reach you first, for it would travel miles across still water. It would begin very faintly, and rapidly strengthen as the canoes knifed towards you, their paddles dipping together into the clean dark water. The closer they came, the louder the young male voices would grow until they passed in full voice 100 yards off shore, still only vaguely visible, and then gradually fade away into the vastness and silence of the great Northwest.

Only when the total silence had returned might you realize that the song you just heard was distinctly happy; that it was sung in French and in perfect unison, and that the rousing singers were happy men, or they wouldn't have been singing at all . . .

There was a time between 1759 and 1798 when very few white men came to the Kaministikwia. This was the period from the fall of Quebec, when French fur trading suddenly ceased, until the Northwest Company bought the land at the river's mouth from the local Indians. During that time, the northwest fur trade was carried on through Grand Portage. Since 1801, when construction of Fort William began, British and French have lived at the Lakehead, although vastly more of the one than of the other.

The singing of traditional French songs continued after 1763 . . .

. . . The closer they came, the louder the young male voices would grow . . .

SETTLEMENT

. . . in 1845, prospectors began venturing into the area, . . .

Ribald songs, spirited dancing, tall tales and other unique performance feats were much in evidence during the yearly Rendezvous at the old fort. Quieter, more gentile music filled the Great Hall when dancing was enjoyed by the gentlemen partners and their Indian women. And at every possible opportunity, tales of adventure and endurance were told by all in their own groups.

There was music, too, through the long winters in both the fort and its adjacent Indian village. Life was very dull during the cold season, and undoubtedly the few Quebecois who remained here after completing their contracts with the Northwest Company, thought of their European roots as they lived with their native wives, or reminisced about their days as voyageurs, and found warmth in such times of loneliness by singing the songs they remembered. Those who remained in the fort, thought likewise, with the same result. Witness the part played by Old Joe, the fiddler, at reconstructed Old Fort William today, and the songs and dances at the Indian village. And of course, the bagpipes.

Following the seizure of Fort William by Lord Selkirk in 1816, the Great Rendezvous abruptly ceased. No longer did several thousand men descend upon the Kaministikwia's mouth every July. Fort William thereafter became just another Hudson's Bay Company trading post, manned by a handful of white men. And so, for many years, the Kaministikwia lay in dormancy.

Then, in 1845, prospectors began venturing into the area, seeking copper, silver and gold. In 1848, Jesuit Father Jean Pierre Chone established the Mission of the Immaculate Conception three miles up the Kaministikwia. John McIntyre and his family arrived from Michipicoten in 1855, to take charge of the Hudson's Bay post, Fort William. He and his family remained here after he retired in 1870, and so the McIntyres became Fort William's first settlers. It was he who persuaded surveyor Thomas Wallis Herrick to lay out the town plot of what is now Westfort, in 1860.

In 1857, the Gladman Hynd Expedition came here to build the Dawson Road. Upon seeking the advice of local Indians as to where best to locate the route, they were directed towards the mouth of the Current River, and thus established the site of what is now Port Arthur. They called it

DEVELOPMENT BEGINS

...Finnish immigration brought choirs and much music...

'The Landing'.

In 1860, John McVicor became our first postmaster, while John McIntyre and Duncan McEachen began mining silver. The same year, Sisters of the order of the Daughters of Mary, came to the Fort William mission, and in 1863, the McKellar family established its homestead near the old fort. By the time Archibald McLauren arrived in 1868, the McKellar homestead was finished, and Peter and Duncan McKellar were mining silver at their Black Bay mine. The same year, Silver Islet was discovered, and the boom was on. It brought such a wave of settlers that by the time Col. Garnet Wolseley landed his troops on May 25th, 1870, headed for Red River, the population already numbered 300. It was he who named the place Prince Arthur's Landing.

Along with these settlers, came their own unique cultural traditions which they quickly adapted to life in the wilderness. Such musical instruments as were available and portable at the time, were brought along for the pleasure they provided. Bagpipes, of course, had long since arrived, and violins, mandolins, banjos, and guitars quite possibly were in evidence occasionally, with mouth organs and concertinas distinct possibilities. As time went on and the settlement grew, organs and even pianos made their appearances, but always, where no instruments were to be had, singing was done unaccompanied, for our early settlers were very fond of song.

The 1870s was the decade in which Thunder Bay's performing arts established their foothold, for it was a time of considerable settlement and cultural achievement. Throughout our history, there was always a larger population in Port Arthur than in Fort William, but the cultural evolution of Thunder Bay depended upon the citizens of both.

Of special note is the beginning of Finnish immigration in the early 1870s, for it has brought several choirs and much music to the Lakehead, along with many outstanding citizens and numerous community contributions. They were our first major group from Continental Europe.

By 1870, Kate McKellar was teaching a school in Fort William. By 1872, a Mr. Goulais was operating a Catholic school in Prince Arthur's Landing, and Miss Alice Warner was teaching 18 protestant pupils as well, and both teachers worked in their own homes. Also in 1872, the Methodists opened the first church in Prince Arthur's Landing, and Jesuit Father

Baxter arrived to establish St. Andrew's Roman Catholic parish.

By 1873, Rev. Mr. McKerracher arrived in Fort William to establish a Presbyterian church, and the first Public School Board was elected in Prince Arthur's Landing.

In 1874, St. Andrew's Roman Catholic church opened in Prince Arthur's Landing. It was later destroyed by fire, and its modern day successor has housed many a presentation of major religious works by the Thunder Bay Symphony Orchestra and Chorus.

The first Lakehead newspapers began publishing in 1875. They were handwritten. The first, called *The Perambulator,* was produced by Peter McKellar and Miss Groom, the teacher. It was printed on a school gelatine tablet, and circulated around the community. It appeared every three weeks beginning in February, 1875, and ceased publication late in that same year.

In Prince Arthur's Landing, a similar publication called *The Thunderbolt,* appeared that same year, edited by George Marks and G. F. Holland. In July, 1875, *The Thunder Bay Sentinel* was launched by Michael Hagen, followed on June 6, 1877, by *The Fort William Day-Book* and *Kaministiquia Advocate.* These latter two were the first to be typeset in their respective towns.

On June 1, 1875, sod was turned on the C.P.R. at Westfort, and later that year, a Dramatic Society was organized at Prince Arthur's Landing. This was also the year in which the Public School Board opened its newly-built school in Prince Arthur's Landing.

By now, Lakehead homes, resembled those of Toronto. Over-sized furniture adorned the rooms, and had begun to include organs, sewing machines, vases, large paintings, drapes and the like. Families enjoyed evening sing-songs around the organ.

Generally, throughout the Northwest, people made their own fun and recreation in whatever way they could. Dances were very popular, and tended to be open affairs. Sometimes you went to public halls, but more often you simply rolled back the parlour rug, called in the neighbours, and had your fun. Moreover, such events were family entertainment, because everybody participated. The old taught the young, and so, by teen-age, every-

1-2

... *people made their own fun* ...

1-2 "Casino Group" — child actors in costume   T.B.Mus.

1-3

1-4

6

1-3 1890 Kaministiquia River picnic party near Ogilvie elevator   T.B.Mus.

1-4 Saturday afternoon gathering outside the Hudson Bay store at the turn of the century   T.B.Mus.

. . . these national community celebrations were born in our barns . . .

THE FIRST PROFESSIONALS

. . . The actors had learned their skills at home . . .

body could dance.

In remote areas, and often even in larger towns, the music was supplied by whoever could play an instrument. The musicians gave their audiences whatever music they had learned at home -- such as *Life in the Finland Woods, the Crooked Stovepipe, The Mason's Apron,* etc. -- and thus contributed their small bit to the development of something that has survived to this day, and is as distinctly Canadian as Kakabeka Falls. It's called square dancing.

Although they're now rather esoteric, these national community celebrations were nevertheless born in our barns, sanctified in our country schools, and hallowed in our lodge halls. The music they inspired sprang from the grass roots of many lands, and their fundamental rhythmns achieve exactly the same results today as they've always done. They make you tap your feet, and want to dance.

The Lakehead had had regular summer steamship service since the Americans opened their canal at Sault Ste. Marie in 1856. On all passenger vessels, it was the custom to provide entertainment and recreation for patrons. Recreation was confined to deck sports, while the entertainment would include dancing, sing-alongs, and even concerts. These were organized affairs, which might nevertheless be rather spontaneous, since they depended upon the passengers themselves, to supply the talent.

Often, a professional or well trained musician or singer happened to be on board, and as time went on, more of such people were found aboard the ships. All of them passed through Thunder Bay, and as construction of the C.P.R. progressed, more and more of them stopped here. They were always welcomed.

By the 1880s, regular dramatic productions were being enjoyed in Prince Arthur's Landing, if not in both communities. The actors were largely amateurs, but they had learned their skills at home. There, especially in large families, spontaneous plays were often performed for an evening's entertainment. Indeed, this custom persisted even into the Great Depression of the 1930s.

But besides drama and dances, such entertainment as concerts, socials, spelling bees, skating parties, snowshoe treks, picnics, hikes, and singsongs were also quite common. The spirits of our people were generally high, because they knew how to amuse themselves and make the best of isolation, and were always eager to contribute to their own entertainment -- a trait that has remained strong in this city ever since. We've always known that if we wanted something done, we had to do it ourselves.

By 1881, the first six Italian families had taken up residence in Fort William. In August of that year, five members of the Sisters of St. Joseph arrived at Prince Arthur's Landing to work in St. Andrew's Parish. Their first task was to take over the school which had officially opened in 1880, and by July, 1882, Sister Vincent had trained a children's choir of 25 voices. They presented their first concert at the school's first commencement, on July 13th, 1882.

In March, 1882, the Dramatic Club staged a production to help raise money for a library. Later that month, the Prince Arthur's Minstrels 'brought down the house' with songs and jokes. On June 19th, the C.P.R.'s Winnipeg-Thunder Bay line was completed at Vermilion Bay, and the first train from Winnipeg arrived here at 1:00 a.m., July 8th.

Thereafter, regular train service allowed people and mail to move freely between Thunder Bay and eastern Canada via the U.S.A. through Winnipeg. And for many years thereafter, it was common to classify local residents as old timers only if they had received their mail by winter dog team.

The arrival of the C.P.R. brought more than just mail. Travelling vaudeville and melodrama could now reach the two communities, and by 1884, such entertainment had become a regular feature at the Town Hall in Port Arthur.

The hall was located at the corner of Arthur and Court Streets, where now stands the Bank of Montreal. According to reports of the time, its entrance was on Court and you went in through two massive oak doors. Once inside, you sat on moveable chairs that were painted a sickly red, and a wood-burning furnace produced so much smoke during heavy winds, that both performers and customers gasped, coughed and rubbed their eyes. Cigars undoubtedly contributed to the smog, because they were very popular in those days, and most men smoked them -- or chewed tobacco. Renamed

1-5 *Port Arthur Citizens' Band leading Labour Day procession down Cameron Street, September 4, 1905 T.B.Mus.*

. . . the Prince Arthur's Landing Minstrels 'brought down the house' . . .

. . . it was common to classify local residents as old timers only if they had received their mail by winter dog team . . .

1-5

THE EIGHTIES

the Prince Arthur Theatre, the Town Hall burned in 1907.

By 1884, Port Arthur boasted a population of 6,000, all crammed into the area roughly bounded by Bay and Van Norman Streets, and from the waterfront back to Algoma. Its citizenry included miners, lumbermen, railway navvies, surveyors, and other transients. There were 36 saloons in town -- nine in Fort William -- and all of them offered the standard live entertainment of the day in frontier fashion, complete with sleeve garters on piano players, and not much else on the girls.

Such groups as the American Four and the Gipsy Oath were featured at the Town Hall. Nobody remembers them today, but they drew enthusiastic crowds a century ago, as did the frequent melodramas; crowds comprised mainly of men, who thought nothing of whistling, cheering or flinging money onto the stage, and occasionally even trying to make off with a live performer. Some succeeded.

By now, the Sisters of St. Joseph had begun giving individual music lessons to selected pupils. This instruction gradually expanded until they were teaching in three locations: their Convent on Algoma Street, their Convent on Miles St., where CBQ radio is now located, and St. Partick's Boarding School at Franklin and Arthur. It is now done entirely at the Avila Centre.

The 1880s was a decade of much church and school construction locally. St. Agnes Roman Catholic Church opened on Brown Street in 1885. St. Thomas Anglican, on Edward, opened in 1888, but was destroyed by fire a few years later, and rebuilt in 1897. St. Andrew's Presbyterian on Brodie Street opened in 1889, and Wesley Methodist, two blocks north, in 1890. First Baptist in Port Arthur began its services in 1892.

All Lakehead churches had large mixed choirs in the early days, several of whom made outstanding oontributions to local music and still do. Many of their members joined mixed choruses which formed in both cities, and contributed as well through these venues. The larger churches hired organists and/or choir directors by the turn of the century, and two or three installed pipe organs of good quality which are still giving service.

During the 1880s, many local schools were built, improving educational facilities and quality, and also widening the incidental artistic

... many were able to inspire a life-long appreciation of the arts ...

THE GAY NINETIES

... Port Arthur residents were taken home by train.

... whoever won a lunch, also got the girl who had packed it ...

training available to local children. A good many teachers came here with extensive backgrounds in music or theatre, and gave their pupils the benefits of their knowledge. Thus, many were able to inspire a life-long appreciation of the arts in their pupils, along with a desire to participate whenever possible. This latter achievement has been an ongoing one, and can be gauged annually in the numerous school concerts held throughout the city by both Boards of Education.

Before the end of the decade, a new wave of immigration brought people of Hungarian, Jewish, Slovakian, and Croatian ancestry to the region. Their descendants have lived here ever since, and have made their own unique and abundant contributions to the culture of the city.

The final decade of the century was one of singing, dancing, ceremonies, and other social affairs at the Lakehead. Having been so extremely isolated for so long, the lodges, clubs, and other groups seemed eager to hold gala social affairs with lots of glitter, music, and food. In Fort William, the Kaministikwia Club was, by now, a social society. It had begun in 1879 as a lobby group, to protect Fort William's business interests, but within a year, had ceased its Chamber of Commerce activities, and become purely a social clique, with regular dinners and dancing.

Many other balls were organized by such groups as the Kedachewin and Shuniah Clubs, and the Mining Club in Port Arthur, and the Masons in both cities. An example of such an occasion was the Masquerade Ball staged by the Mining Club at the Queen's Hotel at Westfort, in 1891. Dancing began at nine o'clock and concluded at 3:30 a.m., following which Port Arthur residents were taken home by train.

Churches were also very active in promoting social gatherings, one of the favourites of which was the box social. This might begin with a variety concert or a short play, but would always end with an auction sale of the lunches. These had been prepared by eligible young ladies before coming to the event, and carefully packed in fancy boxes. These were the objects auctioned off to the highest bidder late in the program, and whoever won a lunch, also got the girl who had packed it. The two could then find a quiet, reasonably public place to sit and enjoy their refreshments, and the church got the money.

1-6

1-8

1-7

Labor Day - Fort William 1906.
~PORT ARTHUR BAND~

12

Arrival of 52nd Batt at Port Arthur Mar 29 1919. Batt moving off on parade

1-9

By now, travelling stock companies produced plays . . .

THE NEW CENTURY

1-6 Dominion Day activities, 1917

1-7 Port Arthur City Band in Fort William, Labour Day, 1906 T.B.Mus.

1-8 Fort William Men's Brass Band T.B.Mus.

1-9 Arrival of 52nd Battalion in Port Arthur, March 29, 1919

Naturally, smart girls made sure the right boys knew which lunches to buy, though there was always the chance that some rich lothario might frustrate them by outbidding the hero. Otherwise, in those restrictive times, box socials were an acceptable way for boys and girls to be publicly private, and give support to the performing arts at the same time. The custom remained very popular well into the 1920s.

By now, travelling stock companies produced plays that brought to Thunder Bay the flavour and music of the Nineties from New York to Paris. These productions, staged in Port Arthur's Town Hall gave zest and excitement to the rapidly growing twin cities. By 1910, over 32,000 people lived here, most of whom enjoyed the nightly vaudeville.

But as well as bringing excitement, the new transcontinental railway took people away with it, and news of the untapped northern wilderness at Thunder Bay, begin to trickle far and wide. As a result, American and foreign tourists began dropping in. One of them, author James Oliver Curwood, was a regular visitor to Port Arthur, and especially to points along the Port Arthur, Duluth, and Western Railway, between 1902 and 1912.

By the 1900s, the C.P.R. had organized a library in Fort William, which contained over 1,000 volumes plus daily papers from Major Canadian cities, and weeklies from Britain and Australia. In Port Arthur, something called the Mechanics' Institute Library was also functioning. These were the beginnings of Thunder Bay's present library system.

In 1900, Chinese immigration began, and the first 20 high school students attended classes in Port Arthur's Central School. They continued there until Port Arthur Collegiate opened in 1909. Fort William Collegiate opened in 1907.

The first Polish people arrived here in 1901. In 1904, the year in which Fort William's Citizens' Band organized, Greek and German immigrants arrived. By 1906, Port Arthur also had a Citizens' Band, and by about the time of World War I, a band also functioned at the Port Arthur Shipyards. This latter group was conducted by Mr. Charlie Mack.

An event of major importance to the future of Thunder Bay's performing arts happened in 1907, when the first 'flickers' were shown to local audiences. These primitive movies caught on as rapidly as did home videos 75 years later, and in less than a year, were nightly attractions. Within the year, local theatres were spicing up their movies with intervals of rapid-fire vaudeville, rather than the other way around, as they had done when the films first appeared.

On Saturday night, November 23, 1907, Port Arthur's Town Hall burned. It had been erected in 1880 and owned since 1897 by the Shuniah Chapter of the Masons, and had been the town's entertainment centre. On the night of the fire, the Western Canada Amusement Company had shown a movie, and moments after the hall emptied, the alarm was sounded. No one was injured, but the building was a total loss. There were, of course, other theatres by then. Within the two communities, they were: the Bijou, the Luna, the original Orpheum, the Lyric, Wonderland, Waddington, Buchta's and by 1909, Fort William's first theatre, the Theatorium on Hardisty Street.

On October 18th, 1909, the new Lyceum opened in Port Arthur. The occasion was marked by a battery of not less than 43 speakers, headed by the Hon. Sir James Pliny Whitney, Premier of Ontario. After the wind had subsided, the real show began, and included Marzella's 60 performing birds; a European comedy bicycle act named Valdore and Varno, two singers and impersonators named La Vere and Palmer; a comedy playlet presented by the Manning Trip; a comedy sketch team of Harris and Beauregard; Florine, the greatest novelty dancer in America; and finally, the latest views of Paris on film. The most expensive seat in the house cost $1.50.

By the end of the decade, two very talented gentlemen had arrived in Thunder Bay, who would have great influence upon the music in these communities. The first, Mr. Ralph Colosimo, came to Fort William with his family in 1907. They had come from Italy, and Ralph was 18 years old. In 1909, Mr. Gunton H. Smalley came to Port Arthur with his family, but he was already a father by then. And of these two men of music, more later.

On September 26th, 1910, the world acclaimed vocalist, Nellie Melba, performed at Wesley Methodist Church in Fort William. Miss Melba, hailed as the greatest living female vocalist, left local audiences with the impression that she was also the world's greatest snob, for she would have nothing to do with local people either before or after the concert.

Something just as ominous to local performing arts as

1-10 Lyceum Theatre   T.B.Mus.

1-11 Orpheum Theatre in Fort William on Archibald and Victoria Streets, circa 1910. The Orpheum entrance was a huge steel and glass canopy lit by hundreds of incandescent globes. The interior was designed in the style of Louis XVI with elaborate relief work and old ivory, woodwork and gold decorations throughout. Draperies were of rich velvet velour in gold and rose. There were 16 mezzanine boxes seating 4 to 6 persons each, with individual flower arrangements in each one. In 1912, the Orpheum was called Canada's most beautiful playhouse.   T.B.Mus.

1-12 Amateur theatrical group, 1888 T.B.Mus.

... The most expensive seat in the house cost $1.50.

motion pictures, made its Lakehead debut in 1910. On October 27th, a demonstration of Marconi Wireless was staged at the Mariaggi Hotel. That evening, the operator talked with a wireless station in Duluth, and with two ships at the lower end of the lake. Since microphones were still far in the future, this demonstration was merely one of wireless telegraphy. Nevertheless, radio had made its appearance and would begin affecting local audiences soon enough.

In 1911, the first Lithuanian immigrants came to Thunder Bay. In 1912, Mr. J.C. Murphy opened the Orpheum Theatre in Fort William. It was the last of the vaudeville theatres to be built here.

1-12

1-10

1-11

Port Arthur Philharmonic Society - Mr. B. Gunton Smalley - Conductor - April 1917

Leadership

B. GUNTON SMALLEY

2-1 *Port Arthur Philharmonic Society with B.G. Smalley, conductor, 1917   T.B.Mus.*

... 'And this time,' he said, 'use your own bow.'"

MR. SMALLEY WAS BORN IN LONDON, ENGLAND, IN 1877, AND WAS A graduate of the Royal College of Music. He and his wife came here in 1910, and settled in Fort William. Local sources say that he was organist and choir director at Wesley Methodist Church, and at First Baptist in Port Arthur, but it isn't clear in what order he served them. He and his family lived, for a time, in the building that is now called the Skihaus.

In 1911, Mr. Smalley organized the Thunder Bay Philharmonic Society, which was a group of music lovers that eventually numbered 98 -- a mixed chorus of 72, and an orchestra of 26. They performed their first concert in 1911, and from then until he left in 1929, the Thunder Bay Philharmonic Society regularly presented major religious works, usually performing in First Baptist Church, Port Arthur. They were all volunteers.

Most of the time, Mr. Smalley was a music teacher, and gave instruction in piano, violin and voice. He called himself the Haydn School of Music, and his studios, when Mr. Arthur C. Manning was a pupil, were up above what is now the Hudson's Bay Store, in the Walker Block on Victoria Avenue.

"I can remember walking there all the way from Ogden Street", says Mr. Manning, "lugging my violin. And then I'd climb the stairs, and he'd be waiting for me, usually leaning half-way out the window, looking down at Victoria Avenue."

"One day when I arrived, he called me over to the window, and so I laid my violin on top of the piano. All he wanted was to give me a nickel to buy him an apple after I played my piece. So I went back to the piano and played, and he just leaned out the window looking at the cars all the time. When I finished, he thanked me very much, and asked if I'd get him his apple, so I put my violin and bow back down on top of the piano, and went down and bought him his apple. I suspect it was for his supper.

"When I came back, he thanked me for the apple, and asked me to play the piece again. 'And this time,' he said, 'use your own bow'.

"Well, that was a shocker! But you know, when I reached for my violin on top of the piano, there were two bows lying there side by side. One was mine and the other his. I don't know how I'd done it, but I had got the two mixed up, and he could tell by the sound, even with his back turned

2-2 Musical production during 16th season of Thunder Bay Philharmonic Society programme   T.B.Mus.

Thunder Bay Philharmonic Society
B. Gunton Smalley, Musical Director
Sixteenth Season

"Nanna Bijou"
"The Sleeping Giant of Thunder Bay"

First Baptist Church, Port Arthur   January 22nd, 1926

2-2

... To help her husband augment the family's meagre income, she played piano at the Colonial Theatre ...

and his head stuck out the window. That's how good he was."

Gunton Smalley and Fred Parish were very close friends, and as is well known, Fred Parish was the founder of the Fort William Male Choir. But, according to Mr. Smalley's only daughter, Mrs. T. Monteith, who now lives in Los Angeles, her father organized and led a group of men called the Westgate Male Choir, which predated our more famous one, and Mr. Parish was a member of it.

Mr. Smalley was also a composer, and through his Haydn School of Music, he presented several recitals in which all the works played were his own compositions. He also led the Port Arthur City Band for a time, and wrote music for that group as well.

Says Mr. Manning, "I have an armful of his music to this day, and it's interesting to see his original inking of the various and many orchestral parts. He was an excellent water colour artist, too, and many of his pictures still adorn local homes."

As though all of this wasn't enough, Mr. Smalley found time to conduct the orchestras at Port Arthur Collegiate and the Port Arthur Technical School (Hillcrest). This is remembered today by Mrs. Eva Giles, founder of the Senior Music Makers.

"He was the conductor at PACI for awhile," she says. "I knew him quite well, and I knew the family. In those days, you had orchestra practices after school. We used to play occasionally at the Collegiate for morning assembly, but at the Technical School, we played every morning. Sometimes they'd just have the Lord's Prayer and a bit of scripture, but everybody would come at nine o'clock, and we'd be playing. We'd play a march when they came in and a march when they went out, and *O Canada* and *God Save the King*. Of course, if there was a longer assembly, we played more.

"But I liked Mr. Smalley. He was a good musician, and his son, Cardo, turned out to be a wonderful musician, too. He married Lettie Lockyer, who lived a few doors from me, so I got to know them very well."

Mrs. Smalley was also an excellent musician. She was a pianist and a choral conductor. To help her husband augment the family's meagre income, she played piano at the Colonial Theatre in Port Arthur.

In 1939, a noted music teacher at the Lakehead, Miss

... Mr. Smalley will always have the distinction of having organized Thunder Bay's first symphony orchestra and chorus...

RALPH COLOSIMO

Therese McAvay, said this about Mr. Smalley's contribution to the performing arts in Thunder Bay:

"Mr. Gunton Smalley laboured (I was going to say slaved, but you can't slave at what you love) with devotion for 20 years. He gave *The Messiah* many years in succession, *Stanford's Revenge,* and *Elijah* with massed choirs, and many orchestral works; but something was amiss. Rehearsals were badly attended; the public was luke warm. His mistake was, I imagine, lack of organization. He tried to do too much. His work was the conducting of the orchestra, of which he was capable. As a business man, like many other musicians, he was, to put it kindly, indifferent."

The Smalleys departed for Vancouver in 1929, because the larger city would provide him with a wider scope of operation, and also because he had relatives there. His son Cardo, already a talented musician, became the Concertmaster in the Vancouver and Victoria Symphony Orchestras, and a violin soloist many times on the C.B.C. He died in 1980, and his widow still lives in Victoria.

Two other sons died at early ages of heart attacks, and Mrs. Smalley died in 1956. Gunton Smalley, himself, died in Vancouver in 1942, at the age of 65. A short time before his death, in December, 1941, he presented *The Messiah* to mark the 300th anniversary of its first presentation. On that occasion, he conducted an orchestra of 100 and a chorus of 150.

Here, at the Lakehead, Mr. Smalley will always have the distinction of having organized what can legitimately be called Thunder Bay's first symphony orchestra and chorus. The fact that he could find so many excellent singers and musicians, attests to the excellence of local music teachers who were his contemporaries, or had already preceded him. And because he worked so well in his own time, and inspired such dedication and support from others, those who followed him found it just that much easier to draw together the talent and expertise to make music.

Many people, over the years, have contributed to the development of the performing arts in Thunder Bay, but undoubtedly one of the most outstanding was Ralph Colosimo. From the time he arrived here in 1907, until his death in 1952, Mr. Colosimo was involved with bands, orchestras, choirs, combos and pupils, and very often with more than one at the same time. Moreover, most of the life that he gave to music was given after working hours, and the key word is *given*.

Ralph was born in the little town of Colosimi, right at the bottom of the Italian 'heel' in 1893. By the time his family decided to emigrate to Canada, there was a good sized Italian Community in Fort William, and so they came here. Ralph was 14 when they landed, and already deeply in love with music.

He had taken his elementary schooling in the old country as well as some musical training, and continued both here. In 1911, he joined the Fort William Italian Band as a clarinet player. In 1913, he joined the Port Arthur City band, and played in it until 1919, when he became Band Master, and led the group for the next two years. During this period, he also re-organized the Italian band to one of 60 pieces and directed it, as well.

And then, in 1921, it became necessary to dispose of the family property back in Italy. Son Ralph was prevailed upon to make the trip overseas. He decided that since he was going back anyway, he would like to extend his musical studies, and was accepted as a pupil by Maestro Vassexla, one of the greatest band conductors in all Italy, at the Academy of Sainte Cecelia in Rome.

By then, he was in his late 20s and had never married. No sooner did he get back to Italy, than he met a young lady, and within six months, they decided to get married. At that point, he made his first contact with the Italian bureaucracy, and was immediately conscripted into the army.

Can you imagine his distress? Here he was, a peaceful, honest young Canadian student, merely wanting to get married and then get on with his studies, and now forced into the army! During the recruiting interview, it was discovered that he was an experienced clarinet player and so, when he reported to the 58th Infantry Regiment at Padua in February, 1922, he found himself playing clarinet in the regimental band. He still wasn't overjoyed, but at least he would have music. And then, while walking around the barracks, who should he bump into but Joseph Fogolin, his old friend from the Italian band in Fort William, and now also a member of the Italian army.

Let Mr. Fogolin continue the story.

"At the end of 1921", he says, "my brother lost his wife,

... At that point, he was conscripted into the army.

PRIVATE COLOSIMO

2-3 Goodsell-Colosimo Dance Orchestra, 1924

and was left with three children. He was in considerable debt, so he asked me to take his kids back home to Mama in Italy. We talked about it, and finally I took them back to the old country.

"But when we got there, we had to register them at City Hall, so they could be schooled in Italian. That's when the army found me, and I was in the same position as Ralph. In fact, I got to the barracks three weeks before he did."

The same long list of questions had been asked of Mr. Fogolin as were asked of Ralph, and because he played the coronet, he also ended up in the Regimental Band. They embraced, when they saw each other, as warmly and naturally as only two heart-broken Italians can really do.

"We played in the band together," he continues, "and then in June, we went on manouvers in the Alps, to a place called the Seven Plains, near Azziago. But in the meantime, our maestro, who also directed two civilian bands in Padua, had to take them to a band exhibition, so he appointed Corporal Major Forti to direct us while he was away.

"Forti was a good enough player, but no band master, so we were all disappointed, because we didn't play the classics anymore. The people over there really love classics, and here we were just playing marches, fox trots, and other light music. Everybody was disgusted. So I said to the others in the band, 'It's too bad, you know, because we do have a really good band master right here. He used to conduct an Italian band back in Fort William, and we played classics all the time.'

"Well, they all got together and talked Ralph into leading us. And when our maestro came back, the Colonel asked him the name of 'that little conductor' who had replaced him. The maestro knew nothing about it, so he asked me, and when I told him about Ralph and what he'd done back home, and how and where he had been studying in Italy, he was a shocked man."

And so, just as Private Ralph Colosimo was about to rise to prominence in the Italian Army, a relative of his new bride arranged for his discharge. The man was a staff officer at Army Headquarters in Rome, and so, after just five months in uniform, Ralph was suddenly a free man. He returned to the Academy of Ste. Cecelia, and completed his studies in harmony, coun-

21

terpoint and instrumentation under Maestro Vessella, returning to Canada in 1923. (Mr. Fogolin had to stay in the army until February, 1923.)

By the time Ralph got home to Fort William, Gunton Smalley was mounting those big choral productions of his with the Thunder Bay Philharmonic Society, and Ralph played clarinet in his orchestra. He also played in the pit orchestras at the *Orpheum* and *Royal* theatres. In 1926, Paramount Pictures sent him to Winnipeg to effect an experiment in seating an orchestra on the stage between pictures. This plan was carried out at the Colonial theatre for six months. At the end of the decade, when talking pictures arrived at the Lakehead, he entered the insurance business, eventually becoming Assistant Manager of Prudential Life in Fort William. This necessary vocation he pursued until a stroke forced him to resign in 1949, three years before his death.

In 1928, his first wife died. He married Miss Ida Bernardi in 1932, and they had six children: Raymond, Gerald, Albert, Murray, Elizabeth and Kathleen.

Following the departure of Gunton Smalley in 1929, Messrs. Kennedy and Phillips tried to recreate the orchestra, but their efforts were frustrated by lack of support. Ralph Colosimo continued with his band work, and sometime in the mid-30s, somebody wanted to hold a Christmas Cheer concert. He was asked to find an orchestra for it.

According to Miss Theresa McAvey, a distinguished local violin teacher at the time, he pulled one together easily, and after one or two rehearsals, the city had an orchestra again. Unfortunately, it was only intended to exist for one performance, so it dissolved with the final number. However, the venture must have convinced Ralph that he could inspire amateur musicians to play like professionals, because he decided, just at the outbreak of World War II, to take the plunge and organize a symphony orchestra of his own.

Miss McAvey describes how it began:

"On Sunday evening, September 10th, I had a telephone call asking me how I'd like to join an orchestra. I asked what kind of an orchestra. Well, the speaker was indefinite, the fact was the orchestra was a wish rather than a reality. 'Couldn't we have a meeting at your studio tomorrow

HIS OWN SYMPHONY

2-4 Kathleen Lee, featured with Colosimo Accordian Band at many of their spring symphony productions

2-4

night and talk things over?' Of course, I was very interested, curious and slightly dubious, but I consented. Out of that phone call and next night's meeting, another orchestra was started at the Lakehead. By started, I mean it actually got underway with a practice the following Sunday, 55 members showing up.

"The group who inaugurated the movement included Charlie Fassel, Hubert Badanai, Don Buchan, Ossian Walli, Tommy Grimshaw and last but not least, Ralph Colosimo, who was the dynamo of the crowd. We unlocked our bosoms, and loosened our tongues, and decided that the need of such an organization in cities the size of Fort William and Port Arthur, was a cultural necessity. We pooled our resources which consisted of some orchestral music and a list of names of capable instrumentalists. It was obvious from the first that Ralph Colisomo should be our director, the man of whom we all naturally thought when an orchestra of any size was contemplated."

The Thunder Bay Concert Orchestra, as it was soon called, acquired a Board of Directors of 12, including N.M. Paterson, as President, and even had some patrons. Maestro Colosimo rehearsed them regularly and the Orchestra performed its first concert at Fort William Vocational School on Monday, December 11th, 1939. Many were the accolades of those who attended, and the full house stood to applaud the 62 musicians at the conclusion. By the next concert, on Monday, February 12th, 1940, the orchestra numbered 71. Mr. Gunnar Wickstrom was Concertmaster.

"Ralph recruited people from all over the two cities," recalls Saville Shuttleworth. "I played for him for a few years, and so did my dad. He had quite a repertoire of the various overtures that both bands and orchestras played, as opposed to symphonic music. He had had a lot of that kind of concert work."

A new member of the orchestra for that second concert, was Mr. Kenneth McKay, who is now Superintendent of Maintenance for the Lakehead Board of Education, and was a young man of 18 at the time. He was studying violin with the Sisters of St. Joseph in those days, and two fellow students -- Mr. Jack McLeod, and Dorothy Taylor -- suggested that he join them in the new venture. He agreed, and when permission was granted by the con-

We unlocked our bosoms, and loosened our tongues . . .

ductor, he came to rehearsals.

"I recall Ralph Colosimo as a firey little guy," he says, "small in stature but quite heavy. And he used to perspire profusely when he conducted, he was so active and agitated. But he was really a wonderful conductor. I can remember new numbers he'd hand out, and I would see they were too difficult. 'Well, we'll see,' he would say, and then he'd take each group by themselves and practice them separately. Sure enough, he'd get us to play something we didn't think we could handle."

The full orchestra rehearsed every Sunday at Selkirk and sometimes at the Ortona Legion, and the separate groups went to Miss McAvey's studio or to church basements during the week.

"I remember one Sunday morning," continues Ken, "we were rehearsing at Selkirk, and I was late getting there. When I walked into the auditorium from the back, the orchestra was playing a Strauss waltz, and it was so beautiful and so good that I just sat down; I just sat there and enjoyed it for the whole time they played. It was that good."

Unfortunately, it didn't last. Ralph Colosimo poured his heart, soul, and a good bit of personal savings into making that Concert Orchestra a permanent one, but the dream had to be abandoned.

There are people around town who'll tell you that the musicians demanded to be paid, and because there was no financial support for the venture, Ralph paid them out of his own resources until he could do so no longer. Others, who actually played in the orchestra, say this may have been so, but that they, themselves received no pay, and expected none. The Musicians' Union -- Local 591 of the A. F. of M. -- received its charter on May 20th, 1938, and was quite strong at the time Ralph Colosimo began his Concert Orchestra. Local musicians were certainly being paid for their services by the end of the 30s.

Mr. Tom Grimshaw, one of the founding players, said in a letter to the editor of a local paper some time after the formation of the Lakehead Symphony Orchestra: "Nevertheless, symphony orchestras necessarily incur expense and upkeep, even without musicians' pay, and all previous efforts in the field of orchestras have failed (here) because of the inability to meet that expense through public support."

24

"I recall Ralph Colosimo as a firey little guy," . . .

. . . Ralph paid them out of his own resources . . .

2-5 (Clockwise from top) R. Waas, N. Biggs, H. Brown — regular entertainers with Colosimo Accordian Band

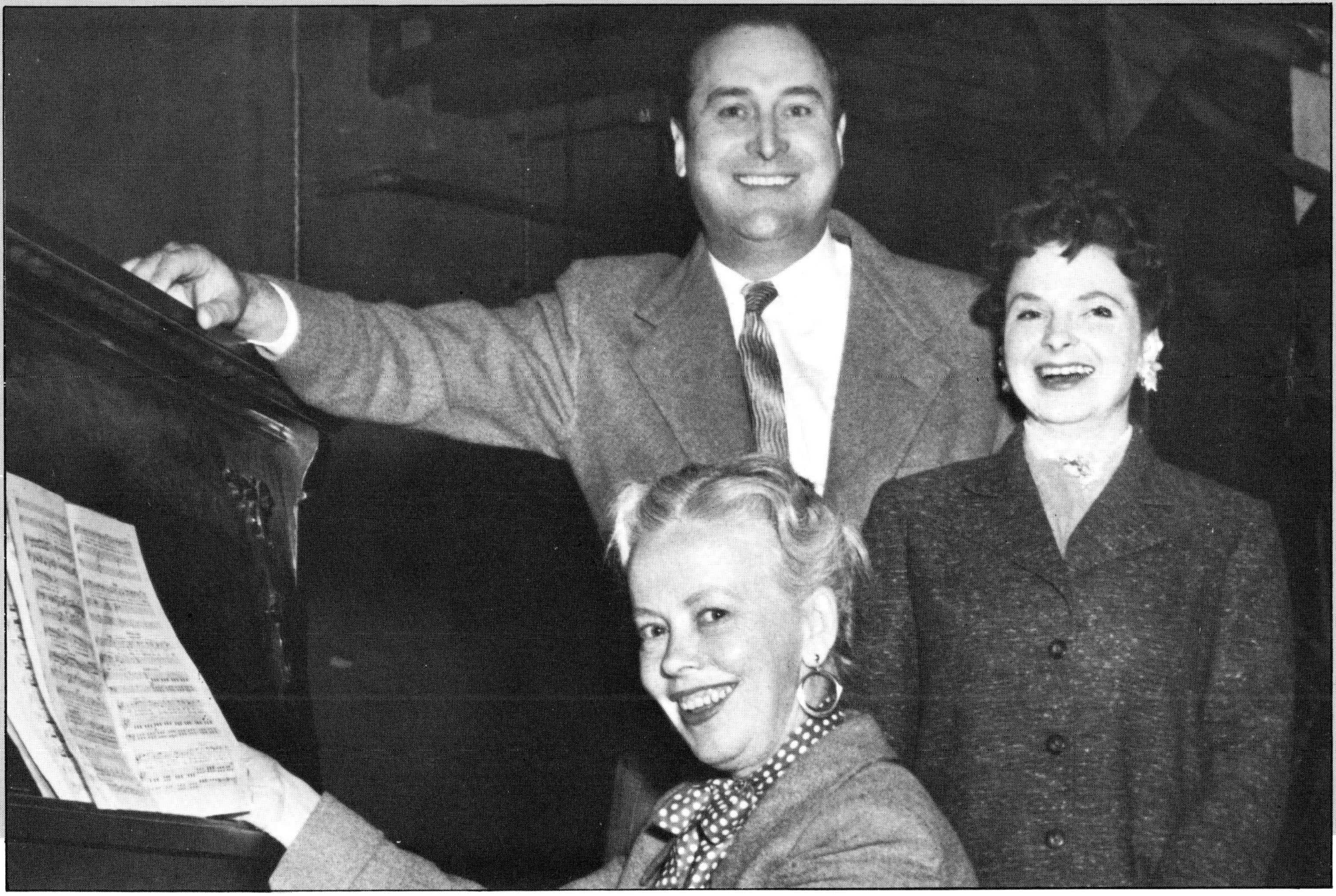

2-5

Which leaves one to speculate that, had Ralph Colosimo received the kind of support that was given to the Lakehead Symphony when it formed 20 years later, he would have died a much happier man.

Mrs. Ida Colosimo, his widow, recalls that her husband formed the Goodsell-Colosimo orchestra which played for all kinds of occasions. He also directed the Fort William City Band, and eventually, the Lake Superior Regimental Band. He often conducted bands in concert on Sunday afternoons at the Chippewa Park Band Shell.

In November and December, 1942, he presented a choir of 60 voices, backed by an orchestra of 25 at St. Dominic's Church in the east end, performing masses.

"We used to have family concerts, too," says Mrs. Colosimo. "After church, out would come the instruments, and we'd hear all our favourite pieces. We'd have musicals, too, with Vince Pungente, and other members of the band, and it would be such fun."

Their son Murray, who is an internationally known musician and now conducts the Ridgewood Symphony Orchestra in Ridgewood, N.J., learned to conduct at those family recitals.

"He liked the clarinet," she says, "and it was Ralph's favourite instrument. Murray wasn't very big, and Ralph would sit him up on his little stool, and there was a mirror, and then he'd say, 'Now Murray, you look up there and conduct. Make sure you conduct just like daddy'. He'd show him how to conduct, and this is why Murray turned out to be a conductor."

In 1949, shortly after leaving Prudential Life, Ralph opened the Colosimo Accordian Studios, and was soon entertaining Lakehead audiences with an annual Spring Symphony, usually held in the Coliseum and featuring all his pupils. Following his death in October, 1952, at the age of 59, Mrs. Colosimo continued the school for several years. By then, too, the family had also opened its music store.

Of Ralph Colosimo, Miss Theresa McAvey said, "As a musician, Ralph Colosimo was a humble servant to his art, genuine, simple and modest. As a man, he was dynamic, methodical and magnanimous. To us, of the orchestra, he was a personal friend. He was affectionally known

THE FINAL YEARS

... Ralph would sit him up on his little stool ...

... Ralph Colosimo was a humble servant to his art ...

WILFRED COULSON

... It was worthwhile coming all the way from New York to hear these wonderful Port Arthur singers."

amongst us as Ralph."

Said Mayor Hubert Badanai, of Fort William: "I have been a personal friend of Ralph's for over 25 years, and during that time he has shown an exemplary public spirit for the common weal. Never thinking of remuneration but concerned always with the things that would give the people enjoyment, such as orchestral concerts."

And from Ken McKay, 33 years later: "He really did seduce performances out of us that we never knew existed. He really did."

Sometime in 1924, a very talented Englishman named Wilfred Coulson formed the Women's Choir of Port Arthur. He had recently arrived from England, and was the organist at St. Paul's Church in Port Arthur.

Mr. Coulson had studied with Plunket Green, who was one of the most renowned singers in England at the time, and so he had had excellent training before he arrived.

As organist, Mr. Coulson was allowed to use the church's facilities for teaching. In addition, he rented a small studio in the Public Utilities Building. He was an excellent organist and choir director, but it's rather obvious that his greatest love quickly became the women's choir.

Their first notable accomplishment at the Lakehead occurred in December, 1924, when a Russian tenor named Vladimir Rosing came to town and sang with them. For the way in which he had brought his choir up to such a pitch of perfection, Mr. Coulson was commended by Mr. Rosing and Mr. Fred M. Gee, an eminent organist who had come here from Winnipeg, especially to accompany Mr. Rosing.

By the spring of 1925, the 42-voice WCPA pleased its director so much that he took them to compete in the Manitoba Music Festival. They sang two pieces, receiving a total of 194 points out of a possible 200, which was better than anybody else did at the festival.

In Winnipeg, the choir competition was adjudicated by a noted personage -- Mr. T. Tertius Nobel of New York. In his remarks at the conclusion, Mr. Noble said, "I consider them more than a choir, for they are an orchestra -- a vocal orchestra if I may so term it. The blending of the voices was beautiful and the altos, especially, were glorious. It was worthwhile coming all the way from New York to hear these wonderful Port Arthur singers."

An audience of 9,000 heard them when they competed again in 1926. This time, they won two outstanding awards. They brought home the Birks Shield and the Ste. Cecilia Shield, having scored an unheard of 99 points on one of their two pieces. There was also a trio of choir members who earned 195 points for their two pieces. These ladies were Molly Mooney, Mrs. E.J.B. Dobie, and Miss Janet Crouch.

In his remarks, adjudicator Hugh Robertson said to Mr. Coulson, "You can tell your choir, and you may use the statement for publication if you wish, you are the finest choir I have heard in this country up to the present, and when at your best, as I have heard you, you are equal to the best we have in England."

Mr. Robertson's praise wasn't the only plaudits earned by the choir at that competition. Mr. Lawrence Mason, music critic for the Toronto Globe and Mail, said they were one of the most outstanding musical organizations in Canada. At the conclusion of the festival, Manitoba's Lieutenant Governor, Sir J.A.M. Aitkens, expressed appreciation on behalf of Winnipeg, and donated $250 towards their travelling expenses.

Shortly after they got home, radio station CKY made arrangements to broadcast them. This was done by special circuit from the Prince Arthur Hotel, in May, 1926, and was aired locally in Winnipeg. (Local papers said 'continent-wide'.)

That, in itself, was a first for Thunder Bay, and very likely in all of Canada. There was no such thing as a broadcasting network in those days. The Canadian Radio Broadcasting Commission -- the forefather of the C.B.C. -- was still nearly a decade away, and radio broadcasting was very much in its infancy. You listened with earphones, and your tuner was a crystal set. Nevertheless, the Manitoba Telephone System did own two broadcasting stations in the early days of radio. One was CKX in Brandon, and the other CKY in Winnipeg, so one presumes that the rental of the necessary high quality telephone circuit was easily arranged for what would obviously have been a highly experimental broadcast.

In 1927, the Lakehead Music Festival was organized, and it was no longer necessary for local artists to compete in Winnipeg. Therefore,

... You listened with earphones, and your tuner was a crystal set ...

ON TO TORONTO

... we couldn't have a big meal before we sang."...

MABEL AIRTH

Mr. Coulson didn't take his choir out of the city for such purposes again. He did, however, take them to Toronto in 1929, at the invitation of the C.P.R., to perform at the official opening of the Royal York Hotel.

The choir left Port Arthur on May 5th, and returned May 9th, and were the only choir to participate. Mrs. Jean Crittall, a member at the time, recalls the trip:

"The entertainers included John Goss from London, and Dame Myra Hess," she says. "There was also a team of Morris dancers. And we were invited, too; all sixty of us. We went by train, and a judge here, I've forgotten his name, gave us $1,000 towards the trip. We filled two cars on the train."

Mrs. Forester, who was also a choir member, still remembers how strictly their director governed them before they sang. "Usually, we could eat only one slice of brown bread and an apple, which we had to chew very carefully," she says. "But at the Royal York, we were allowed some fruit salad. But we couldn't have a big meal before we sang."

Mr. Coulson's only income in Port Arthur, was his organist's stipend and whatever he earned in teaching, and so he found it necessary to leave.

"My father was a minister at the time," says Mrs. Crittall, "so I know how hard it was financially. I remember Wilfred Coulson coming to visit him, and going over all his problems. What could he do? How could he stay? He loved that choir and this community, because it was here that he had built the greatest choir of his life, but he couldn't make a living. So he accepted what was known as the Chalmers organ in Ottawa's Challenge Church. He and his wife and daughter came with us to the Royal York, and from there, he went directly to Ottawa."

There, he developed another excellent choir, which successfully competed at the Eisteddfod in Wales. Eventually, he and his family went back to Scotland, where he died.

For the Women's Choir of Port Arthur, the trip to the opening of the Royal York was a climax in more ways than one. Not only did it signify nation-wide recognition, but it also looked very much like it would be their last public function. Their Director didn't return with them, and a choir of

2-6

2-7

2-6 *Port Arthur Women's Choir with Wilfred Coulson conducting, 1925*

2-7 *Lydian Ladies' Choir with Mabel Airth conducting, 1950*

. . . sitting beside her made it almost possible that I could sing second soprano."

such obvious talent, would not simply disband and quit singing.

Two conductors from out of town, were found to lead the group for a time, but the successes achieved by Mr. Coulson were never realized again. Eventually, one of the choir members, Mrs. Mabel Airth, could see that the group was disintegrating, so she gathered together the remnants and created the Lydian Ladies Choir in the early 30s.

In 1933, the Lydian Ladies sang with the Fort William Male Choir at the Norman Room of the Royal Edward Hotel, in support of the Times-Journal's Christmas Cheer Fund. There were undoubtedly other concerts, and the choir certainly competed in the Lakehead Music Festival.

Mrs. Shirley Gerow, remembers Mabel Airth:

"She had been in the Women's Choir of Port Arthur," she says. "She also sang duets with Mrs. Dobie from time to time. I started taking lessons with her in the fall of 1947, and she was a marvellous teacher. She was the one who decided that I was a meso, and not a coloratura soprano.

"She was organist and led the choir at St. Paul's in Port Arthur, and I sang with her at weddings and the like. My mother, Mrs. Forester also sang with her.

"The last time I sang in the choir, she made me sing second soprano, and that meant I didn't sing the tune at all. That's always rough on somebody who has always sung soprano. So I sat beside Jean Crittall. We used to practice in PACI, and the two of us would sit in one of those double desks, and sitting beside her made it almost possible that I could sing second soprano."

Mrs. Airth directed the Lydian Ladies Choir until 1954, when it disbanded. She was a distinguished vocal teacher, organist and choir director at the Lakehead for many years, and a very strong supporter of the Lakehead Music Festival.

She died in 1971, and for a time was annually remembered at the Festival through the awarding of the Airth Rose Bowl to the vocalist earning highest marks.

The Rose Bowl is now presented annually by the Fort William Male Choir to the highest achiever among vocalists and instrumentalists.

3-1

Choirs

OUR SINGING TRADITIONS

3-1 First Male Choir, 1930
Back Row: J. Pickering, F. LeGassick, H. Ede, E. Elvish, W. Polhill, A. Manning, W. Poulter, Mr. Fairbridge
Front Row: S. Hillyer, G. Marks, W. Mackereth, F. Parish (conductor), J. Booth, S. Bishop, Dr. Strachan, J. Hodgson, A. Wyatt

THE FORT WILLIAM MALE CHOIR

THE EXISTENCE OF ORGANIZED CHOIRS IN THUNDER BAY HAS BEEN a fact since churches were first established here. And as the various ethnic groups immigrated, and brought their cultures with them, several were quick to establish ensembles of various sizes and compositions.

Singing was often taught in local schools, too. The first school choir was directed by Sister Vincent in 1882. For a time after World War II, as many as 120 school choirs competed in the music festival. Moreover, the choirs that appeared there were only the ones that local music directors felt had the best chances of winning, which means that at least that many more existed back in the classrooms.

It shouldn't be surprising, therefore, to find 15 choirs currently functioning around the city. Indeed, the wonder is that there aren't more. Here's what we have right now:

The Fort William Male Choir; the Lakehead Choral Group; the Sweet Adelines; the Barbershoppers; the Folklore Group Croatia; the Laus Deo Choir (Dutch); the Otava (male Choir and the Oras (female) Choir (Finnish); Les Troubadours du Norois (French); the German Folksingers; the Alpini Choir (Italian); the Polish Millenium Choir; the Barvinok Singers (Ukrainian); the Ukrainian Carpathy Choir; and the Prosvita Ladies Choir (Ukrainian).

Regrettably, it is impossible to give detailed histories of all the choirs that exist or have ever existed at the Lakehead. Therefore, the following choices have been made, not to suggest that one is somehow better than another, but very pragmatically because these histories were most easily obtainable.

Back in 1927, the men's club at St. Paul's Anglican Church in Fort William, invited somebody to speak to them about the Russian Royal House. The solemnity of the event suggested that suitable musical entertainment also be included, and so eight men formed an octette and sang *The Song of the Volga Boatman*. Today, nobody remembers much about either the address or the speaker, but the successors of the octette are still going strong.

Now approaching its 60th year of singing, the Fort William Male Choir is recognized as one of the best amateur choirs in Canada.

The original eight, all members of church choirs, were: Vic Bird, Ernie Cambridge, Hec Ede, Harry Moorey, Wilf Poulter, B. Roberts, Alf Wyatt, and Fred Parish. The latter served as the group's conductor.

Born in England, Mr. Parish came to Canada as a boy and in 1912, became Chief Clerk in the C.P.R.'s local Freight Department. During World War I, he served in the band of the Cameron Highlanders, and later helped his friend, Gunton Smalley organize the Westgate Male Choir. He was also choirmaster of St. Paul's Anglican Church for 31 years, and served the First Baptist Church of Fort William in the same role for a time as well.

When the Lakehead Music Festival organized in 1927, Mr. Parish was its first secretary, and held that post for 20 years. He was also First Vice-President of the Canadian Federation of Music Festivals, and for his festival work, received the Queen's Coronation Medal. He directed the Fort William Male Choir until 1937.

For the first couple of years, the Male Octette rehearsed weekly in members' homes or wherever they could find a piano. Dues were five cents per practice. Public appearances were few, but thoroughly enjoyed, although audiences were small. The men even made one out-of-town appearance at Kakabeka Falls, and presented a one-hour concert.

In 1930, the original octette was augmented by friends who had asked to join, and in May, the group entered the Northwestern Ontario Music Festival. To their delight, they took first class honours and as a result, decided to organize formally. The Fort William Male Choir was officially launched on June 14th, 1930, proclaiming as its purpose, to promote interest in male chorus singing and in general to foster interest in lakehead musical culture.

The new FWMC's first concert was given at the old Fort William City Hall on November 28th, 1930, with Fred Parish conducting and Jim Booth accompanying. The choir had grown to 28 members, and made quite an impression on the audience.

In 1933, the choir made its first international trip -- to Grand Marais, and also began its many local radio broadcasts over CKPR. Before the end of the decade, it was being regularly heard nation-wide on the C.B.C.

3-2 *Fort William Male Choir, 1954*

... *Dues were five cents per practice* ...

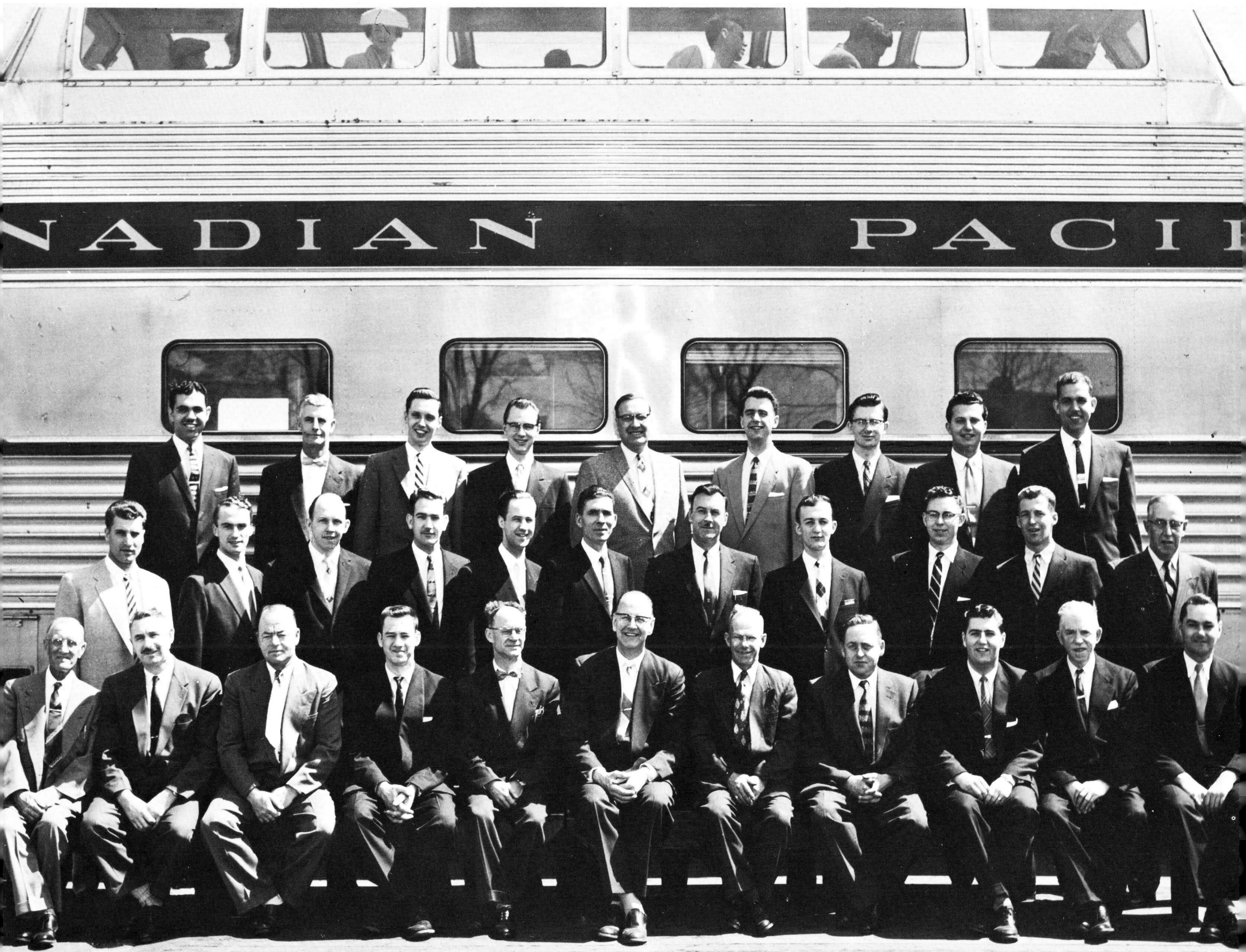
NADIAN PACI

3-3

3-4

FORT WILLIAM (ONTARIO) MALE CHOIR

... In 1946 the choir resumed operations under the leadership of Norman J. Kleven ...

INTERNATIONAL RECOGNITION

3-3 Fort William Male Choir sing for the the opening of Ontario Winter Games 1975, at the Fort William Gardens

3-4 Fort William Male Choir lighting Christmas hearts, 1959

During World War II, enlistments and shift work made rehearsals difficult, so the choir suspended operations for the duration. Up to that point, there had been three conductors: founder Fred Parish, Jim Booth, and J. Wilkie Haynes. In 1946, following an 18-month recess, the choir resumed operations under the leadership of Norman J. Kleven -- the man recognized as having done most to build the choir.

Born in Sprague, Manitoba, Mr. Kleven received his early education there. He studied choral direction in Winnipeg, Toronto, and at the Eastman School of Music in Rochester, New York. He began his teaching career in Fort Frances, and was hired by the Fort William Board of Education in 1944, as Director of Music.

In 1961, he was appointed Master of Music and Psychology at Lakehead Teachers' College, and also served for 11 years as lecturer in music methodology at the Ontario Department of Education summer school in Toronto. He adjudicated music festivals throughout Manitoba and Ontario, and retired from the Male Choir in 1978. He died in Albuquerque, New Mexico, January 25th, 1980.

In 1951, the FWMC joined the Associated Male Choruses of America, and has participated in that organization's annual Big Sings ever since. These take place in a different 'member' community every year, and takes the choir as far afield as Milwaukee and Winnipeg. Thunder Bay hosted the massed choirs' event in 1954, 1960, 1967, and 1978.

However, the choir has also sung many times to audiences elsewhere. In 1961, they were flown to Toronto to provide the official entertainment at the Kiwanis International Convention in Maple Leaf Gardens. In 1963, the men participated in the International Eisteddfod at Llangollen, Wales. In 1976, they sang as part of the Cultural Olympics in Kingston, and in 1984, returned to the Eisteddfod.

This is a group that enjoys travelling, and has made many trips to Europe. Over there, they sing wherever they can, and such spontaneous concerts are usually much enjoyed by their listeners. They are mostly not booked in advance, but occur in parks, pubs, restaurants, or wherever else the choir happens to be when they feel like singing.

The Fort William Male Choir is often asked to participate

in special local or regional events as well. For instance, in 1973, the men sang for Her Majesty, Queen Elizabeth II, at the official opening of Old Fort William, and for Pope Paul VI at his summer residence. But their most distinguished achievement was to have been selected as Canada's Centennial Choir at St. John, N.B., in 1967.

...the men sang for Pope Paul VI at his summer residence...

The FWMC -- a group of approximately 50 voices -- regularly opens Thunder Bay's Yuletide season with its Prelude to Christmas. In February, it hosts a three-night Smorgasbord and Singalong at the Da Vinci Centre, and makes many short appearances for community functions and service clubs all over the city. The choir's performances are always done entirely from memory, and can be sampled on any of its 11 recordings.

Since 1978, Mr. Kendall House has directed the Fort William Male Choir. Ken came to Thunder Bay in 1953, and joined the choir in 1954. He served as its assistant conductor for 12 years prior to being chosen to lead it, and like the founding director, he also conducts a church choir. In Ken's case, his other choir is the successor to the one Fred Parish directed at the Fort William Baptist Church. The buildings have changed, but it's the same choir and congregation -- a generation or two later.

Accompanying the choir at the piano, is Mrs. Diane Crocker. Diane is the only woman member, and the only member allowed to use music during performances. She has been with the choir since 1963, and is now a life member.

...Diane is the only woman member...

Diane also conducts a choir. When she isn't accompanying the FWMC, she directs the Sweet Adelines.

THE LAKEHEAD CHORAL GROUP

Like one or two other choirs in Thunder Bay, the Lakehead Choral Group began because a small group of singers got together and performed at the music festival. This time, it happened in 1956, two years after the disbanding of the Lydian Ladies Choir. James Jewitt was the instigator, and became the founder of a choir that has pleased local audiences with its songs and shows ever since.

Mr. Jewitt, by then, had established a reputation in choral work. He had come here after the war, upon his release from the R.A.F., and was teaching music in the elementary schools here-abouts. In fact, at one time, Jim was an itinerant music teacher, who visited something like a dozen area schools each week; places like South Gillies, Kakabeka Falls, Slate River, and so on. And he taught quite a bit of singing in his travels. He was also Assistant Conductor of the Fort William Male Choir for a time, and one of its frequent soloists, as well as being organist and choir director in a local church.

The Lakehead Choral Group held its first concert on December 13th, 1957, at the Port Arthur Technical Institute, and these shows have been held annually ever since, usually at Selkirk or the University Theatre.

During its history, the LCG has undergone changes in name as well as format. From 1963 until 1965, it was known as the James Jewitt Singers, and became the Lakehead Choral Group again in 1965, when Mr. Jewitt left it to take charge of the music department at Westgate Collegiate. Since then, the choir has performed over 100 concerts and sing outs of various kinds.

In 1967, the LCG joined with the Lakehead Symphony Orchestra, the Cambrian Players, and the Lakehead Music Festival, to form the Lakehead Amateur Musical Productions, and staged five shows: *Brigadoon*, as a Centennial project; *Oklahoma* in 1968; *Kismet* in 1969; *My Fair Lady* in 1970; and *Guys and Dolls* in 1971. The idea behind the LAMP was that the Symphony supplied the musicians, the LCG provided the singers, Cambrian Players looked after acting and directing, and the Lakehead Music Festival took on publicity and advertising. All five productions were highly successful, and extremely pleasing to local audiences.

In 1970, the LCG headed the parade of supporters campaigning for a new Arts Complex, and over the next two years, contributed some $1,200 towards the early groundwork on the project.

Beginning in 1974, the Choral Group has staged at least one major musical production per year. As a result, Thunder Bay music lovers have enjoyed: *The New Moon, The Merry Widow, Die Fledermaus, Brigadoon, Fiddler on the Roof, Carousel, Finian's Rainbow, The Most Happy Fella, Pajama Game*, and *The Gondoliers*, and looks forward to many more in the years ahead.

For a couple of years in the mid-70s, the choir presented mid-winter or spring programs called Moods in Melody, and since 1977, has

3-5

3-5 *The Jim Jewitt Singers, 1963, became known as The Lakehead Choral Group in 1965* T.B.Mus.

39

3-6

3-8

3-7

THE LAKEHEAD CHORAL GROUP PRESENTS

FINIAN'S RAINBOW
from the book by E.Y.Harburg & Fred Saidy; lyrics - Harburg; Music - Burton Lane.

dramatic direction
Tibor Feheregyhazi

music direction
Jim Whicher

Lakehead University Theatre
8:00 p.m.

May 8-10th
-12-16th

3-9

staged an annual Festival of Christmas. There's also Choralfest in the fall, and since 1980, a yearly Show Stoppers.

The choir has also presented *The Messiah* three times, and partook in the productions of Beethoven's *Choral Fantasy* and *Verdi* with the Fort William Male Choir and the Thunder Bay Symphony.

Like other local choirs, the Choral Group often visits senior citizen residences, and performs at other community functions throughout the city.

Since its founding, the LCG has had six conductors prior to James Whicher. They were: Jim Jewitt, Barbara Kirkup, George Warne, Phil Cotton, Jack Nevins, and Sheila Ash. Mrs. Kirkup directed at two different times, and Mr. Whicher took over in June, 1976, He has now conducted the choir longer than anyone else.

The choir has also enjoyed the services of several accompanists: Marg Johnston, Allen Vickers, Doug Dahlgren, Jim Metcalf, Helen Bruzas, Jennifer Rhine, Barbrea Philp, Jeremy Fiorito, Marilyn (Olson) Johns, Judy Martin, Joy Latimer, Joan Black, Diane Potts and Barbara Severen.

The Lakehead Choral Group rehearses in Confederation College's Nursing Building located on Lakehead University Campus, every Wednesday evening throughout the music season.

In 1971, Ken and Pam Duke moved to Thunder Bay from Brandon. Up in Manitoba, they had been involved in Barbershop Quartet singing, and when they discovered that the Lakehead didn't have any, they decided to get something organized. Ken started promoting the idea, and the 'Northern Notes' received their charter on February 16th, 1973.

As with all other Barbershop Quartet groups in North America, they're linked to an international association. Their motto is *We sing that they shall speak,* and their concert profits go to aid logopedics, the science that deals with afflictions which inhibit speech in children and adults.

Since they formed, the Northern Notes have been directed by the late John McCullough, and by Joe Vanderwees and Ted Sayer. Mr. Stuart Kirkup is their present conductor.

The local Barbershoppers sing at many local events, community functions and service club banquets, and stage an annual concert

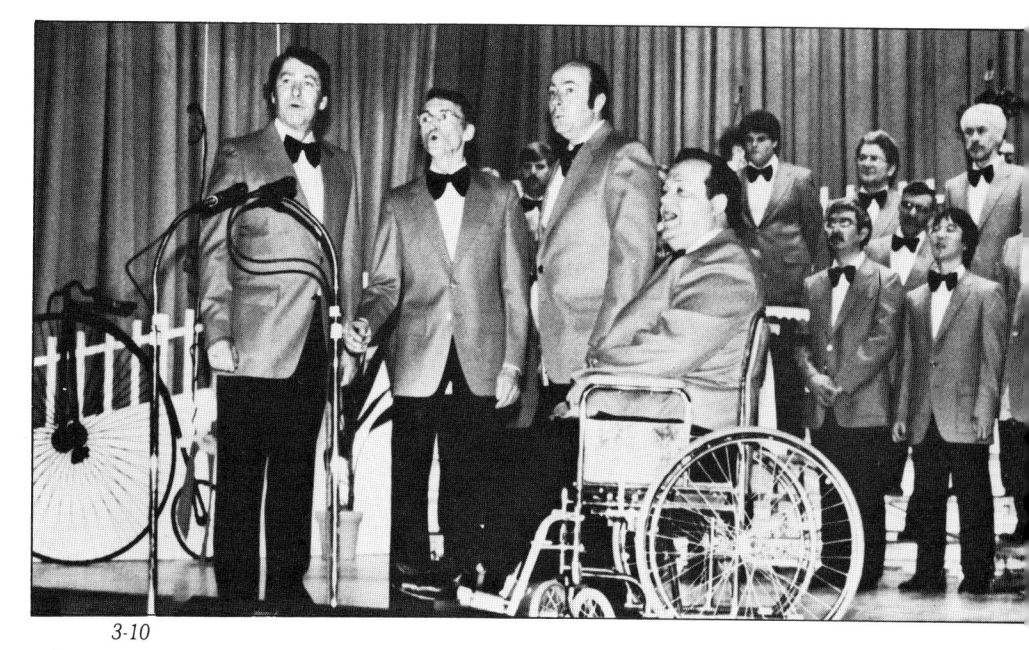

3-10

THE BARBERSHOPPERS

3-6 *Lakehead Choral Group presenting "My Fair Lady" during 1970 season*

3-7 *"Carousel" beach scene performed by Lakehead Choral Group at Lakehead University, 1980*

3-8 *Quintet of Jim Jewitt Singers harmonize in a hit from the show "Oklahoma" TB.Mus.*

3-9 *Lakehead Choral Group enlists Magnus Theatre director Tibor Feheregyhazi*

3-10 *"The Velvet Touch", one of the quartets of the Thunder Bay Barbershop Chorus, performs in Selkirk Auditorium, 1983*

THE SWEET ADELINES

3-11

FOLKLORE

CROATIA

THE LAUS DEO CHOIR

3-11 Sweet Adelines with Diane Crocker conducting

every spring. They also have two quartets which sometimes work independently, called The Velvet Touch, and The Gentlemen's Accord.

In 1973, when the organizing of the Barbershoppers was in its final months, Mrs. Pam Duke held a coffee party at the Prince Arthur Hotel, inviting any women interested in singing barbershop music. She was delighted when over 30 showed up.

As a result, the local group called the Sweet Adelines, received its charter on August 26th, 1974. As with all other such choirs, its purpose is to teach and train its members in singing four-part harmony, barbershop style, unaccompanied.

Like their male counterparts, the Sweet Adelines are part of an international association which boasts 33,000 members all over the world.

The group takes part in regional competitions, sings at local hospitals and social events, and has sung on at least one occasion with the Fort William Male Choir. In November, 1984, they staged their first successful stage show, which was called Better than Broadway.

One independent quartet has now formed within the group, which is called Short and Sweet.

The present director of the Sweet Adelines, is Mrs. Diane Crocker.

It is not possible to detail all the various choirs and small ensembles that exist or have existed in this city, because it would entail many local churches, community groups and ethnic societies. Thus, among those that have or have had higher profiles are these:

The folklore group Croatia is one of two such ensembles organized in 1976 by Father Ilija Puljic at St. Andrews Church. The singers, along with a tamburitza orchestra and dancers, perform usually at the Folklore Festival, but may be seen at other times in the city. They rehearse Wednesday evenings at the Croatian Church on Oliver Road.

A little bit of old Holland blossoms here through the Laus Deo choir. It's a mixed chorus of over 30 voices, which rehearses at the Christian Reformed Church out at Twin City Crossroads.

The Laus Deo was organized by Joe Vanderwees in 1952.

At that time, there were only 10 singers, but the choir has since grown to its present size of over 30 voices. The group maintains a policy of singing at least one number in the Dutch language at every performance. It is primarily a Christian church choir that likes to keep its ties with the old country, but welcomes singers who are not Dutch.

When Joe Vanderwees stepped down as Conductor, the choir was led for awhile by Mr. Fred Brooks. Its present director is Mrs. Alice Wice.

The Laus Deo choir has performed for Princess Alexandra, at the Centennial celebrations in Toronto in 1967, and at the ceremonies marking the 25th anniversary of the liberation of the Netherlands by Canadian troops, in Ottawa in 1970.

Locally, they have performed at the Lakehead Music Festival, the Ecumenical Hymn Sing, Dawson Court, the Lakehead Psychiatric Hospital, and the Folklore Festival.

The city's two Finnish choirs are called Otava and Oras. The first is entirely male, and the second entirely female. Both are conducted by Mrs. Anja Haavisto.

The Otava choir began in 1938 as a mixed chorus, but became exclusively male in 1952.

Oras was organized in 1946, also as a mixed choir, but in 1970, became a ladies choir. This group is unique because it is the only Finnish ladies' choir in Canada.

During the summer, Oras performs at Old Fort William. Throughout the year, it takes part in many functions whose proceeds help local hospitals and senior citizens' homes. It also helps celebrate such special Finnish occasions as Finland's Independence Day, December 6th; Kalevala Day, February 28th; and the Finnish Canadian Grand Festival on the July 1st weekend.

Both Otava and Oras rehearse weekly at the Finlandia Club on Bay Street, and give performances at the Folklore Festival.

The Polish Millenium Choir was established in January, 1966, to celebrate 1,000 years of Christianity in Poland. Initial membership was 10 men and 16 women, and over the years, the choir has performed at many

The Laus Deo choir has performed for Princess Alexandra . . .

FINNISH

POLISH

concerts locally and in Fort Frances and Red Lake. It has worked very hard to establish its good reputation in the community.

This choir, which is affiliated with the Canadian Polish Congress and the Polish Singers Alliance of America, performs regularly at the Polish Independence Day concerts on May 3rd, at Remembrance Day ceremonies, and at the Folklore Festival. It rehearses Thursday evenings during the music season at the Royal Canadian Legion Hall on Simpson Street -- the Polish Legion. Membership is open to anyone over 18, who is willing to sing Polish.

Choir meetings are conducted in Polish and English.

This small ensemble was formed in 1976 by Mrs. Sheila Ash, and functioned until she left the city in 1980.

Originally numbering seven, it grew to 10 mixed voices, and was a study group as well as a performing one. They rehearsed in Mrs. Ash's home, and usually performed in the Public Libraries by invitation. Their repertoire, usually sung unanccompanied, was madrigals and other folk songs suited to small groups. Their only major production was Handel's *St. John Passion*, which they performed at the Fort William Baptist Church in April, 1979.

The Studio Singers was funded very largely by the Thunder Bay Foundation -- through the Thunder Bay Historical Museum Society. When it disbanded, its music was given to the museum, to be used by any other group that wishes, and its funds were turned over to the Lakehead Music Festival to provide an annual award to an adult vocal group.

Members of the Studio Singers at various times were: Sheila Ash, George Campbell, Janice Bick, Henry and Evelyn Konrad, Beth Babion, Marion Henderson, George Hosegood, Bill French, Harry and Margaret Reichman, Sybil Dubois, and Sylvia Beach. For the performance of the *St. John Passion*, the singers were accompanied by Mrs. Marcella Smithers.

Somewhat like the Studio Singers, this group concentrates on performing madrigals and other period music for small groups. It was founded by Miss Elizabeth Ganiatsos, who is a teacher with the Lakehead District Catholic School Board, and was constituted in November, 1981, as a non-profit organization.

3-12 Prosvita Ukrainian Carpaty Choir celebrate their 25 year history

3-13 Opera "A Country Girl" directed by Grace E. Boyle, 1921 T.B.Mus.

THE STUDIO SINGERS

3-12

THE CONSORTIUM AURORA BOREALIS

The CAB has a Board of Directors of eight: Chairman Herman Dost, Vice-Chairman Robin Smith; Secretary Diana Pallen; Treasurer Ken Morrison; Music Director Elizabeth Ganiatsos; and Fred Ball, Wilma Ayre, and Leonard Weaver.

Some of these Board members perform with the group, whose size varies with each project. Miss Ganiatsos chooses the programs and brings in whoever she needs to help.

They've already done old English and French music, accompanied by recorders and drums; a King Henry VIII concert; Bach Cantatas, and the like. They've also twice presented the Pergolesi *Stabat Mater* with strings, and in 1984 did the Handel coronation anthem *Zadoc the Priest*.

At various times, the CABs have been augmented by Jim, Mary and Monica Whicher as well as others. They often perform at Lakeview Presbyterian Church on Cameron Street, but have also sung at the University and at the National Exhibition Centre -- now becoming recognized as having excellent acoustics for small ensembles.

The group was initially funded by the Thunder Bay Foundation and the Port Arthur Rotary Club, and in 1984, raised money to purchase the only two-manual harpsichord in town. It was built by David Jenson, in Winnipeg, a manufacturer who turns out four such instruments per year.

As has been detailed in the chapter on the Symphony, the Thunder Bay Symphony Chorus was organized in the 1970s, and is entirely a volunteer group. It wasn't the first such chorus to be formed here, but this one is very much alive, and obviously in excellent voice. It performs as many as four major productions per year, and numbers some 120 mixed voices.

The fact that our two founding cities have had such exceptional choirs in the past, is at least partly because of the excellent school music programs that intensified after World War II. There had been bits and pieces here and there since the founding of the schools, but nothing like the 20 years immediately after 1945.

Arthur K. Putland was music supervisor for the Fort William board in the 1930s, but he was only half-time in the position. In 1939, Fort William hired Mrs. Hazel Murie, as a fulltime supervisor in the elementary schools. She worked with Mr. Putland until he left in 1943, and then did the

3-13

THE THUNDER BAY SYMPHONY CHORUS

SCHOOL SINGING

... there was no instrumental music taught in schools ...

... The two cities each needed a week to present all their young singers ...

work herself until Mr. Norman J. Kleven was hired the following year.

Between the two, a course of study was developed and implemented through the Fort William system, which began musical training in Grade 1, and progressed to four-part harmony in Grade 8. According to several teachers in the city, this program was entirely vocal, because there was no instrumental music taught in schools until later.

"It was a complete course outline," recalls Glenn Duguid, a former principal with the Lakehead Board. "And you were expected to follow it. Norman Kleven and Hazel Murie devised it, and if a teacher wasn't a musical person, they provided assistance. Every kid took it."

Because of that program, there were a great many school choirs developed each year, and about half of them entered the music festival. The two cities each needed a week to present all their young singers, because there were similar training programs in both systems.

It should be pointed out here that one of the most outstanding choral teachers in either city was Miss Mary Campbell, who taught music in Port Arthur Collegiate for many years prior to World War II. PACI year books of the time are filled with pictures of Miss Campbell and her choirs, because they usually took top honours at the festival.

The choral program continued in Fort William elementary schools until 1961, when Mr. Kleven moved to the Lakehead Teachers' College. Mrs. Murie retired in 1969, and by then, instrumental music was highly developed throughout the secondary schools.

Today, although there are excellent music programs in all city schools, the choices are much wider, and the old insistence upon everybody singing the same song on the same day has vanished. Instrumental music begins in Grade 7, and all the high schools have bands and small ensembles that are really of professional calibre. In fact, many a local high school musician has joined the union before graduating. Also, especially in the elementary grades, folk singing and other musical ventures are available, depending on the expertise of the individual teachers. Recorders, ukeleles, and harmonicas are but three extra instruments that are occasionally taught to entire classes.

In addition, operettas and other musical productions are regularly presented in both the elementary and secondary schools. Christmas concerts, especially in rural schools, are events often requiring latecomers to stand. High school 'Cabarets' and other presentations frequently bring the general public into the facilities, not just the parents of the performers.

But the hey day of the school choirs seems to have passed, and consequently, there aren't as many singers moving into the various performing groups around town. Indeed, when 'Performance' was written, the city was actually short of tenors. What we're tending to get in the 80s, is a growing crop of first class instrumentalists, heading to the bands, orchestras and small combos. And that's because of the excellence of the high school music programs.

3-14 I.O.D.E. production of "The Mikado" T.B.Mus.

3-15 "The King of Cocos Isle" played at Selkirk Vocation School 1948, F. Parish conducting St. Paul's Anglican Church Choir T.B.Mus.

3-14

3-15

4-1

The Dance

... known throughout central North America as one of the best Native Indian dance groups ...

4-1   Early dance group   T.B.Mus.

IT'S FAIRLY EASY TO GET THE IDEA THAT THERE ISN'T MUCH serious dancing going on in Thunder Bay. That's probably because we rarely see big productions of dancers, backed by an orchestra. Actually, there's a lot more dancing being done here than most of us may realize, but we don't notice it because it isn't pushed at us. It just shows up every so often, and usually where we aren't expecting to find it.

We bump into it at the Folklore Festival and at Old Fort William on special days, but we're so used to seeing it there, that we may tend not to notice it. It's also visible fairly often in our malls. Sometimes it crops up at the Music Festival, or in the musical productions of the Choral Group, and certainly at school concerts and programs. And of course, it happens at Thundershell, during Summer in the Parks.

In fact, dancing has been part of our local culture since settlement began, and today there are something like 14 specialized ethnic dance groups in the city. Even more outstanding, there are no less than 10 serious dance schools functioning here.

The Lyon's Dance Troupe formed in 1972, and its 25 members are known throughout central North America as one of the best Native Indian dance groups now practising. Students begin when they're just nicely old enough to walk, and are taught the traditional dances all the way through childhood. The troupe members make their own costumes, and rehearse weekly at the Indian Friendship Centre.

The Vesnyanka Dancers regularly thrill us with their costumes and traditional Ukrainian dances. They formed during Centennial year. Mr. Joe Zurba got the idea, gathered a group together, and brought in an instructor from Winnipeg. This troupe also starts teaching three-year-olds, as does the Veselka Dancers, which is yet another Ukrainian group.

But there's more. The Croations have dancers, as do the East Indians and the Portugese. The Finnish dancers call themselves Kiikurit. Les Troubadours du Norois study traditional French dancing, the Budapest Dancers are Hungarian, and the La Stelle Alpini Dancers are traditional Italian. Three Polish organizations perform their national dances in Thunder Bay: The Fort William Polish Women's club, St. Casimir's Language School, and the Polish Youth Club.

Scottish highland dancing has been seen at the Lakehead for most of two centuries, considering that it was often part of Rendezvous festivities at Fort William. Today, highland dancing is taught by the Morgan's School of Highland Dancing and by the Gayle Hutton Dance School, and the music may be provided by members of our four local pipe bands.

Serious dance instruction got started hereabouts, around the time of World War I. The first instructor was Miss Grace Ensworth, who came from England and operated a classical ballet school. There had been dancing prior to this, but it had all been ethnic.

Of Miss Ensworth, Sylvia Horn (now Mrs. Sylvia Young) says, "I don't know where she got her training, but her work was so good, that when you saw her shows, you knew she could teach. Also, she was very expensive, She charged $1.50 per half hour, which was very high in those days. So, when my father decided to give me lessons, he told me to make sure I knew what I was doing, because this was a lot of money."

In those days, too, the occasional school teacher had dancing experience, and passed it on to her pupils.

"I had a phys. ed. teacher," says Amelia Jackson, "who taught us different little dances, like the highland fling and things like that, which I already knew, but it was fun to participate."

Next came a lady named Mrs. Ally. She had been Mrs. Camfield, but had remarried. She came to town and auditioned children for shows that she put on in the Lyceum Theatre. This would be just after World War I., and she put on a different show each summer. Sometimes, the productions had an ethnic flavour, but she did operettas as well, and many children participated.

"I remember an older girl who was my baby sitter," recalls Miss Horn. "She talked my mother into letting her take me to the audition. I'd be three or four at the time. But I got a part, doing something called *Freckles*, and from there, I got the feeling that I wanted to dance."

Around this time, a third teacher, Mrs. Mona Stewart arrived with her son and two daughters.

"She brought more variety into dancing," recalls Mrs. Jackson. "She took more interest in teenagers, whereas the others had dealt

... Scottish highland dancing has been seen at the Lakehead for most of two centuries ...

THE BEGINNINGS

... She charged $1.50 per half hour

4-2 *Miss Sylvia Horn performs "Fairy Queen" in a Grace Ensworth recital held at the Orpheum Theatre, 1925*

with younger children."

In those days, dance teachers didn't have to be certified, and if students wanted to pursue careers in dance, or to take further studies in it, they had to leave town. Often, they had to leave the country, especially if one's desire centred around classical ballet.

"That was the time," says Amelia Jackson, "when, if you wanted major examinations in ballet, you had to go to England. And after the war, when inflation went way up, you just couldn't afford such things. So you struggled as best you could."

Both Mrs. Jackson and Miss Horn studied in the United States, and Miss Horn also studied with Nicholas Legat in London, taking Russian ballet. Both -- like most other serious dance teachers here -- continued their professional development through seminars and special courses, long after being certified.

"I felt that those two beginning teachers had done a lot," says Mrs. Jackson. "Then I went to Gladys Height's School of Dancing in Chicago, and she was world travelled at the time. She had been a prima ballerina and had had a number of teachers who were introducing the modern dances as well as acrobatics. She also taught stage direction."

Amelia Jackson and Sylvia Horn began teaching dance at the Lakehead at about the same time -- at the onset of the Depression. Amelia Jackson is now Principal of the Dance Centre of Northwestern Ontario, and Miss Horn operates the Sylvia Horn School of Dancing and Baton. Both women are certified by the Canadian Dance Teachers' Association.

But among dancers and dance teachers, much attention is given to whether or not a teacher has been trained in the Cecchetti system (Chu-KETT-y). This is a system that progresses a student in definite stages which, although gradual, aren't easy. Each year, certified examiners adjudicate each student in each stage, and the pass mark is 80%. In all, the process can take about 10 years to complete, but if the student wants a career in ballet or in teaching ballet, it's the only way to get it. Accordingly, the instruction begins in early childhood -- about age five or six -- and is completed in early teens, at which point, the decision can be made whether or not to pursue dancing as a career.

4-3

4-3 *The national dance, Krakowiak, is demonstrated by Polish dancers at the Folklore Festival, 1975*

4-4 *'The Adagio Team' who performed locally in the 1930's were trained by Amelia Jackson*

4-5 *Debbie Delvecchio wins top marks for her Hungarian dance at a 1965 competition   T.B.Mus.*

4-6 *East Indian dancer*

4-4

4-5

4-6

4-7

4-8

4-9

4-7 *Traditional dance performed by Lyons Dance Troupe*

4-8 *Lyons Dance Troupe at Mount McKay participating in "Mahmoowaydidaing" or 'gathering', 1980*

4-9 *French Canadian dancers*

"It's the most recognized form of training for classical ballet students," says Amelia Jackson. "And it's the basis of all other dancing."

Not all local teachers instruct in Cecchetti, and it isn't difficult to understand why. After all, not every dance student goes on to serious career dancing. Indeed, most of them decide very early to dance as a recreation or hobby. And so, while it may be well to have a child begin with Cecchetti, why continue it if the interest wanes? Why insist that the pupil be taught Cecchetti or nothing? Hence, the various local schools and dance courses.

But for those with definite possibilities, it is important that the right things be taught at the right time, and to that end, it was decided to establish an organization which could officially draw upon the expertise available throughout the country.

"Betty Goodings and I decided that since we both taught Cecchetti, we should bring in examiners," says Amelia Jackson. "This led to our calling a meeting of local professional teachers early in 1964, and we were chartered on March 25th, 1964."

The aims of the Northwestern Ontario Ballet Guild are to increase appreciation of the ballet; to promote its teaching to the highest possible standard; to provide scholarships for promising students at national schools; and to present before the public, performances of ballet.

Since its inception, the Guild has sponsored an average of five workshops per year. At these workshops, students from all area studios receive superior training under nationally-known instructors. Each summer since August, 1964, the Guild has organized and operated an annual summer school of dance, at which students may study ballet, character or modern dancing. The Guild has also sponsored yearly ballet performances, the most outstanding of which have been the appearances of companies such as the full National Ballet Company.

"Most of the local teachers at the time", says Mrs. Jackson, "had received only the training from their original teachers. They hadn't gone out of town, so they really didn't have the knowledge of what students need, nor did they seem to understand that as the teacher progresses, the whole thing progresses. We had auditions here for the first time, because of the Guild. The National Ballet came here and auditioned 10 children to take to their school that first year, and this sort of thing can encourage you to take further study. Because, if your student is accepted by the NBS, you know you're on the right track."

The Guild also presented ballet for children, locally, with such productions as Nutcracker and Sleeping Beauty. The idea is to promote the dancing, and provide opportunities for young dancers to be seen. The emphasis, of course, is on proper instruction and Mrs. Jackson cautions parents against enrolling their children in short dancing courses offered in conjuction with other recreation courses.

"What's happening," she says, "is that young people who may have only taken a year's training, are offered temporary jobs teaching kids to dance, and they don't know how to teach dancing. They don't know what they should be teaching."

Sylvia Horn echoes this sentiment. She says, "I've had girls come to me saying that they have to do a number, but every time they do a particular step, it's hard for them. Well, that's because they're being given steps that are too advanced for them. Their instructors haven't got the background of the different years of training."

The certification that qualifies dance teachers can come from any of several dance bodies, but the good ones come only after very rigid examinations.

Once a person qualifies, of course, he or she can confidently begin teaching the art. And like every other teacher of any subject, the good ones have excellent young people to show the public in due course.

"We have recitals," says Sylvia Horn. "At one time, we had a show every year, just for the parents. It was very seldom that the public could be invited, because parents are always so proud of their little five or six-year-old, that by the time you let in all the aunts, uncles, and grandparents on both sides, all the seats have been taken. We used to hold them out in the schools."

There are also the ballet productions done by the Guild, and a growing number of situations -- such as the Lakehead Choral Group's productions -- where short scenes involving dancers occur in the scenarios.

. . . if your student is accepted by the NBS, you kow you're on the right track . . .

4-10 Majorettes prance on stage at the Finnish Hall

4-11 1964 Summer School with Betty Oliphant, principal of the National Ballet School correcting Rosalie Dicks at the barre. Carol Chadwick demonstrates

4-10

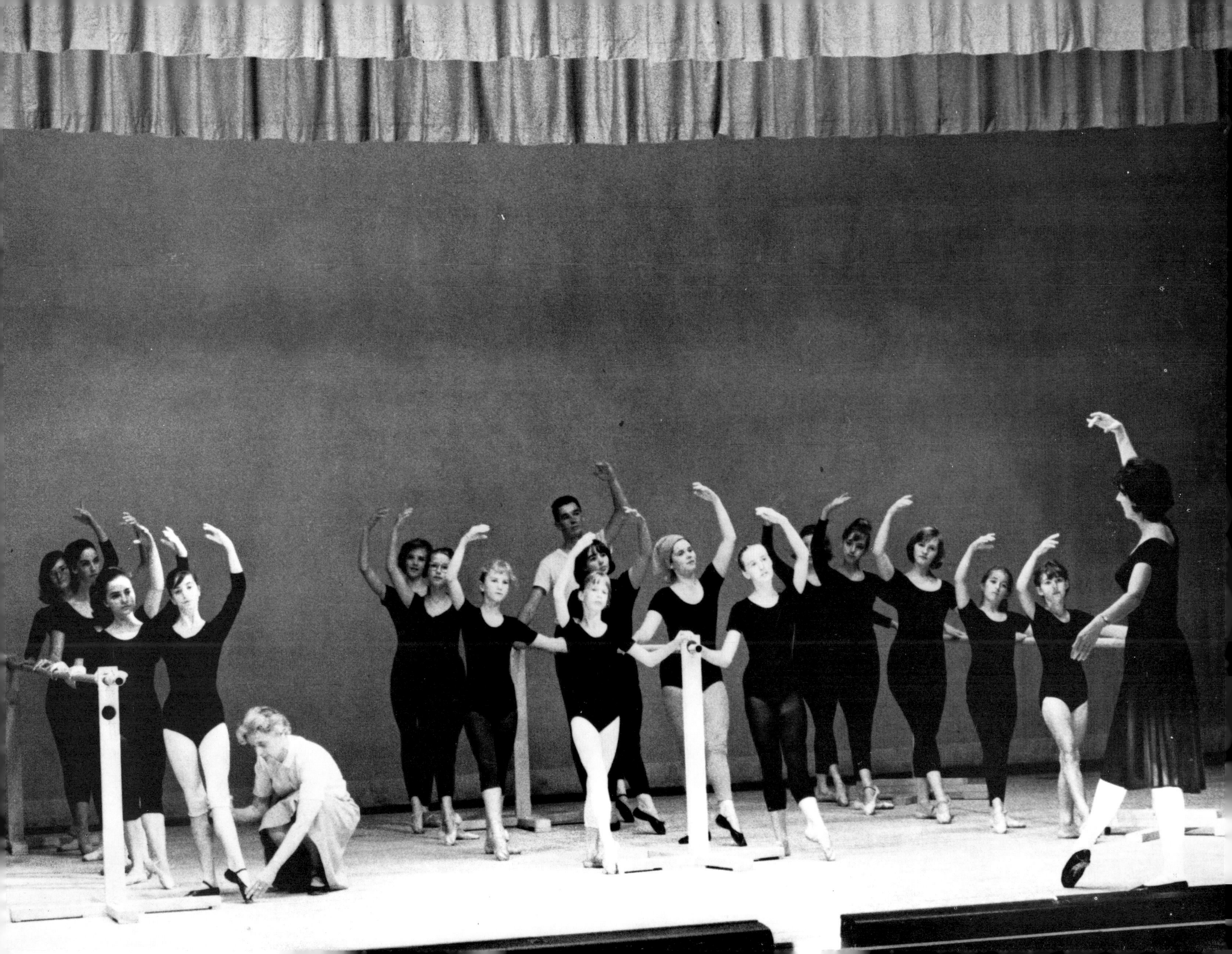

THE SANTA CLAUS SHOWS

4-12

Here, young dancing students are not only welcomed, but eagerly sought.

And in the past, some very large local productions have been staged, such as the annual Santa Claus Show that used to be sponsored by Chapple's.

"Grace Ensworth started them," says Miss Horn. "She originated them with Mr. Chapple, Senior. I was a little girl, and that was my first show. I'd be about eight or nine. It was a Saturday morning at the Orpheum. Three shows -- 9, 10, and 11; all children, and of course, Santa came too. They didn't give gifts at first, but it was a lovely show; generally a fairy story about Santa coming in and walking the dolls."

Following Miss Ensworth, Gladys Hartley took it over, and eventually, Sylvia Horn. Miss Horn staged the first two at the Orpheum and then Chapple's asked her to take it over to the Fort William Gardens.

"I had always complained that there wasn't enough room in the Orpheum," she says, "so Norm Himble asked me if I remembered Chautauqua. Well, of course I remembered it. My father used to take me, and it was a great big tent that had a square stage."

He asked her to prepare a similar presentation for the Gardens -- a big square stage in the centre, with lots of activity on it and around it. Chapple's would build whatever stage she wanted, and everything else she needed.

"What a challenge for a choreographer!" she says. "Everything had to be back-to-back. I'd have to do everything in squares. Whatever happened facing east, had to happen facing west at exactly the same time!"

Throughout the fall, performers were chosen, scenarios written, music selected, costumes made, and scenery constructed.

"And can you imagine walking on ice in ballet shoes?" she says. "But we did it. All the way around, and when Santa came up on stage, oh, the children! They used to bring them in; thousands of kids . . . ten thousand . . . all tied together in groups, because if they ever wandered away, you'd never find them! . . ."

They did Alice in Wonderland that first year. Miss Horn was up at 4:30 in the morning, getting everything ready for the two shows -- one at nine, and the other at 11.

Of course there were problems, as there always are in any production. For one thing, the band had to sit away across the ice, and there had to be blackouts. She depended upon the music, whose timing had to be razor sharp. Because of the communication distance, the timing was usually out, and remained that way for several other shows, until it was solved in a unique way.

"Jack Masters did it," she says. "He was the disc jockey at CKPR at the time, and he and I worked together for years. I'd go up to the studio, with all the show in order, and he would tape it. The year we did The Wizard of Oz, I did Dorothy's voice, and as many of the vocals as I could. We'd work till two in the morning, but on the day of the show, Jack would run the tape, and it was absolutely precise. Beautiful!"

They held the last one in 1972.

Now that the Auditorium has opened, Thunder Bay should see dance productions a bit more often, and by outstanding world performers like the Royal Winnipeg Ballet and the National Ballet School, and others. Such programs will certainly foster our appreciation of the art, but whether or not we actually see local dancers in big local productions depends upon more than one organization combining efforts. This has certainly been done around the city before -- in Lakehead Amateur Music Productions -- so hopefully, the precedent has been set for other similar projects.

Meanwhile, let us watch those youngsters in our malls and wherever else they appear. They're receiving excellent training at Thunder Bay's dancing schools. They are very talented young people, and some of them will undoubtedly go places, since there's now a future in dancing in Canada.

4-12   *Chapples' Santa Claus show was held at the Fort William Gardens*

4-13   *Here comes Santa himself*

4-13

5-1

Drama and Theatre

Drama and Theatre

OLD THEATRES AND MOVIE HOUSES

..."When you see what you saw when you came in, the picture's over."...

5-1 "The Masque of Empire", 1908
T.B.Mus.

5-2 D.W. Griffin's newest film appears at the Lyceum Theatre

5-3 Foyer in the Lyceum Theatre   T.B.Mus.

5-4 Lyceum Theatre interior
T.B.Mus.

5-5 Lyceum Theatre interior
T.B.Mus.

ALTHOUGH IT'S DIFFICULT TODAY TO DETERMINE EXACTLY WHERE the old vaudeville theatres were located in our two cities, they were all here by the start of World War I. Such names as *Lyceum, Bijou, Luna, Orpheum, Lyric,* occur in news reports of the times, along with *Palace, Corona, Rex, Royal* and *The Town Hall.*

By the time of silent movies in the 1920s, young men could enjoy an evening on the town with their girl friends, for about $1.50. That bought them both a movie, refreshments, and car fare downtown and back.

In Port Arthur, the *Colonial* was located on Red River Road, next to McNulty's. The *Lyceum,* opposite the Prince Arthur Hotel, still carries that name at the top of the building. In Fort William, the *Royal* stood next to the St. Louis Hotel, and the *Orpheum* across from Chapples, on Victoria Avenue.

The first theatre built in Fort William was the *Theatorium.* It stood on Hardisty Street, and opened in 1909. It eventually had a sign in the foyer which read, "When you see what you saw when you came in, the picture's over." In 1912, the *Orpheum* opened. The *Corona* stood on what is now a vacant lot south of the Royal Edward Hotel, and was opened in 1915. About 1914, the *Royal* was built on Victoria Avenue, and the *Rex* stood near the West Hotel on Simpson Street.

Both the *Orpheum* and the *Lyceum* had been originally built for stage productions, and were equipped with box seats called 'loges'. Of the two, the *Orpheum* was the more luxurious, with lodges at the balcony level down both sides of the auditorium. It also had red and gold plush curtains which opened and closed at the beginning and end of movies.

Talking pictures came to Thunder Bay in September, 1929, and opened in both cities simultaneously at midnight showings. Then it was found that the old theatres had been very well built in terms of acoustics.

After being closed for a decade, the *Lyceum* reopened in 1934, and for a short period, old time vaudeville was featured between showings of movies.

During the Depression years, to compete with the advent of radio, movies had Dinnerware nights. These usually happened weekly, and

5-2

GRIFFIN'S LYCEUM

No Advance in Prices For This Special Christmas Program

No Advance in Prices For This Special Christmas Program

Special Christmas Offering Monday - Tuesday - Wednesday

MATINEE 2.15—EVENING, 7:00—9:00

David Wark Griffith

The World's Greatest Producer, Who is Responsible for Such World Famous Successes as

"THE BIRTH OF A NATION," "BROKEN BLOSSOMS" AND "THE HEARTS OF HUMANITY"

Presents His Supreme Triumph

Girls !!!
Read This

WHICH IS THE GREATEST LOVE?

Of all the loves, which is greatest in your mind?

Some people say the greatest love is that of a mother for her son.

Others believe it is the love of a father for his daughter.

Still others contend that the love of the bachelor for his pipe or his dog, or the child for her puppet dolls, the maiden aunt for her parrot, the miser for his money, are greater than all other loves.

Greater love hath no man, it once was said, than that one man should be willing to give his life for his brother.

Which do you believe is the greatest love? See "The Love Flower," the D. W. Griffith sensational United Artists production.

AT THE LYCEUM MON — TUES— WED.

Here was a girl who knew no fear — who looked Death in the eye time and again to save one she loved from the vengeance of the law. A Story of Love and Sacrifice — of Romance and Adventure —

DAVID WARK GRIFFITH'S newest picture **The LOVE FLOWER**

From the Collier's Weekly Story "Black Beach" by Ralph Stock

THE GREATEST LOVE AND ADVENTURE STORY EVER WRITTEN

ON THE SAME BILL WITH THIS SUPERB FEATURE

CHARLES HUTCHINSON, in "DOUBLE ADVENTURE"

CHESTER COMEDY, "HOLY SMOKE"

KINETO REVIEW

LAST SHOWING TONIGHT OF

HARRY CAREY in 'The Wallop'—LARRY SEMON in 'The Fall Guy'

DON'T MISS THE LAST CHAPTER OF "VANISHING TRAILS"

5-3

5-4

5-5

5-6

5-7

5-8

5-9

63

5-10

5-11

5-12

5-13

5-14

5-15

for the price of admission, you received a piece of chinaware -- a cup, saucer, plate, or bowl. The idea was to come each week and collect the entire set in a few months. Many people did, because movies were so regular and so cheap.

Vaudeville, of course, died by the outbreak of war, and over the years, the old theatres were torn down. In their places, new ones rose, and were eventually divided into more than one movie house.

At last count, in Thunder Bay, there were 21 movie screens functioning.

As already noted, Thunder Bay's first dramatic society was organized at Prince Arthur's Landing in 1875. It isn't clear as to when one got started in Fort William, but it's obvious that there has been at least sporadic interest in acting and theatre in this community for over a century.

According to an article by the late Mrs. Christina Wright, in *The News-Chronicle* of February 28th, 1953, a serious drama group called the Lakehead Little Theatre Community Players organized about 1923. Headed by James Clofs, it included J.A. Royce McCuaig and Miss Helen Roenicke. Its director was Laura Goodman Salverson, a local writer. The group produced *Madam Verite at Bath*, *Exit Columbine*, and *Mountain Road*, which Mrs. Salverson wrote.

In all, this group numbered 20 people. They produced their plays at the Technical School, and once in the dining room of the Prince Arthur Hotel, but their activities lasted for only a year and a half.

Several years later, the Masquers Dramatic Guild of Port Arthur and Fort William came into existence. It was headed by Alfred Goodrich, and its directors were Miss Pearl Sparling and Christie Dunbar.

The group included Annette Kyle, Dorothea Greening, Arthur Moore, James Main, Jack Hunter, Henrietta Brown, Edity Petts, Morris Desourde, Gladys Carter, Olga Kirkup, Mrs. Carl Sorenson and Sidney Landau. Their productions included *You Can't Take It With You*, *The Optimist*, *Smilin' Through* and *Street Scene*, and they gave a special presentation of the latter for the employees of Canadian Car and Foundry during World War II.

In 1949, the Community Players of Port Arthur was formed with Harvey Bradley, a high school teacher, as its head. By then, the

5-6 Actors pose on stage of the Finnish Hall, Bay Street

5-7 Cast of a play directed by Mr. Heckley on stage of Finnish Hall

5-8 Play performed by the Finnish actors during the Great Depression

5-9 Cast from operetta "Hainen Eski" which was staged 1930-31

THE CAMBRIAN PLAYERS

5-10 Chautauqua's Martin Erwin Players present "Smilin' Thru", 1927 T.B.Mus.

5-11 The international programmes presented by Chautauqua brought entertainment to early city audiences that was previously reserved for cosmopolitan patrons of the performing arts T.B.Mus.

5-12 "Chautauqua" was an all-Canadian institution of travelling performers T.B.Mus.

5-13 The Colonial advertizes adult admission at 40¢ and includes special orchestral music

5-14 "Too late for the early show" T.B.Mus.

5-15 Colonial Theatre, 1940 T.B.Mus.

5-16

... the total conversion cost was in the neighbourhood of $90, ...

5-16   Child actors in costume
T.B.Mus.

Provincial Government provided organizational assistance, through Arthur Clare of the Department of Education. Among the members of the first executive were Jim Main, Eileen Williams, Clifford Morrison, Eleanor Drury, T.W. Thomson, and Murray Chercover, with directors Edity Petts and J.I. Garvey. Other directors over the years included Marion Bell, Gladys Carter, Harvey Bradley, Edity Petts, Christie Dunbar, and Peter Evodkimoff.

Besides producing plays, this group studied staging, lighting, and make-up. They met for a time in the Oliver Road Community Centre, then at the Technical Institute, and then at the Nursery Warehouse at Current River.

In the latter location, the group was able to build and paint flats, build the pieces of scenery and assemble their lighting equipment, but they couldn't erect sets, nor was there storage space. Moreover, the floor wasn't large enough for rehearsals.

Accordingly, the group abandoned these quarters, and for a winter, met in members' homes. In the spring of 1952, they acquired what they imagined would be their permanent home, and moved there. It was an old church, large enough so that even 12-foot flats could be built. There was also a storage area, and plenty of room to work and rehearse.

Mrs. Dusty Miller recalls the place:

"It was the old St. Michael's Church on Red River Road. They had built a new one and were moving into it, and they told us we could have the use of that little church for awhile. We were very happy about this.

"We converted the place into a marvellous little theatre. We spent hours of work on it. You have no idea. I think the total conversion cost was in the neighbourhood of $90, because everything was scrounged, loaned, or given to us. We got donations of lumber and we all worked. People would come in on a Friday after work, and work Friday night, all day Saturday and all day Sunday. We used to bring meals to them, just because we were scared that if we ever let anybody go home, he or she wouldn't come back.

"An enormous task! We even got some old seats that had belonged to a movie theatre, and they were either donated or we paid $10 for the lot of them. The place held about 100, so we scraped the rust off them and repainted and recovered them and did a whole job, you know. It was fantastic.

...the church was going to require that space for a parking lot...

"The university invited all the arts groups to come together with them..."

"Well!! After all of this, we were told after about a year that, unfortunately, the church was going to require that space for a parking lot, and we would have to move out. And I cannot tell you what a blow that was!! It's a wonder we didn't just fold up."

But they didn't. Indeed, they actually produced plays during that year, and by the spring of 1953, had been invited to participate in the Manitoba Regional Festival in Winnipeg. With financial assistance from the community, they took On Monday Next to Winnipeg with its cast of 12, where the play was presented for adjudication, and was well received.

However, when they were evicted from the building on Red River Road, they were without a home until Lakehead University built its theatre.

"The university wanted to get a lot of community support for its building," says Mrs. Miller, "so they invited all the arts groups to come together with them, and they set up a kind of little arts council of their own. By then, too, a lot of the people from the Fort William Little Theatre had died or left town, and a smaller group was left there. Some of the other people joined the Community Players of Port Arthur, so what was happening, in effect, was a kind of amalgamation without any particular direction to it. It was just starting to happen.

"Well, the university didn't want to have a group come in which was associated with only one city, and of course, we were talking amalgamation at this time, so we had a meeting and created the new name -- The Cambrian Players. This was in 1963."

By the spring of 1985, the Cambrians had produced their 100th play, and had worked very hard to acquire their national reputation for excellence. They are still an amateur theatre company, but one which consistently produces professional quality theatre, and they not only produce plays, but hold workshops to train their members -- and others -- in all aspects of theatre.

"The Cambrians are unusual," says Dusty Miller, "in that long before there were any grants, we would put on workshops and pay for them ourselves. We brought in professional directors and so on, and this is still highly unusual for any organization.

. . . They took the play 'All My Sons' to Winnipeg and won top honours . . .

"We were involved in the Dominion Drama Festival, which has been very important for the nurturing of theatre in Canada. In fact, there wouldn't be theatre in Canada, except in isolated little pockets, if it hadn't been for the DDF in those early days."

The first time the Cambrians attended the Dominion Drama Festival -- although they were the Community Players of Port Arthur at the time -- was in 1958. They took the play *All My Sons* to Winnipeg and won top honours. Early in 1978, they presented *The Ecstasy of Rita Joe* at the Theatre Ontario Festival in Oshawa, and brought home awards for best production, best leading actress, best supporting actor, adjudicator's award for special achievement, and four honourable mentions. *All My Sons* was directed by Dusty Miller, and *The Ecstasy of Rita Joe* was directed by Betty Inksetter. The latter had a fairly large cast, several of whom were native people, who, with other members of the cast, had never acted before.

Because of their willingness to study the background of theatre, the Cambrians have an extensive knowledge of the field. This expertise is willingly shared with other performing groups throughout the city, and so it's quite common to find Cambrians behind the scenes in most of Thunder Bay's amateur productions. And all of that help is given voluntarily.

The Cambrians supplied the back-stage crews for the first two operas done by the Thunder Bay Symphony Orchestra. They were a major reason why Magnus Theatre survived its formative years. They always helped the Lakehead Choral Group, and were an important part of the Lakehead Amateur Music Productions in the mid-60s. Prior to that, the Cambrians were instrumental in organizing the Lakehead Summer School of Fine Arts from which came the Lakehead Council of the Arts, and ultimately the Thunder Bay Arts Complex Committee. They knew exactly what was needed for the performance of stage productions in Thunder Bay, and made their suggestions very early in the campaign.

Over the years, a goodly number of Cambrians have moved into professional acting. Susan and Joy Chapple, Don Jamieson, Nancy Josie, Joel Kramer, and Stephen Taylor among others. Both the Chapples are or have been professional actresses. Don Jamieson, who chooses to live in Thunder Bay and regularly performs at Magnus, has also been seen in

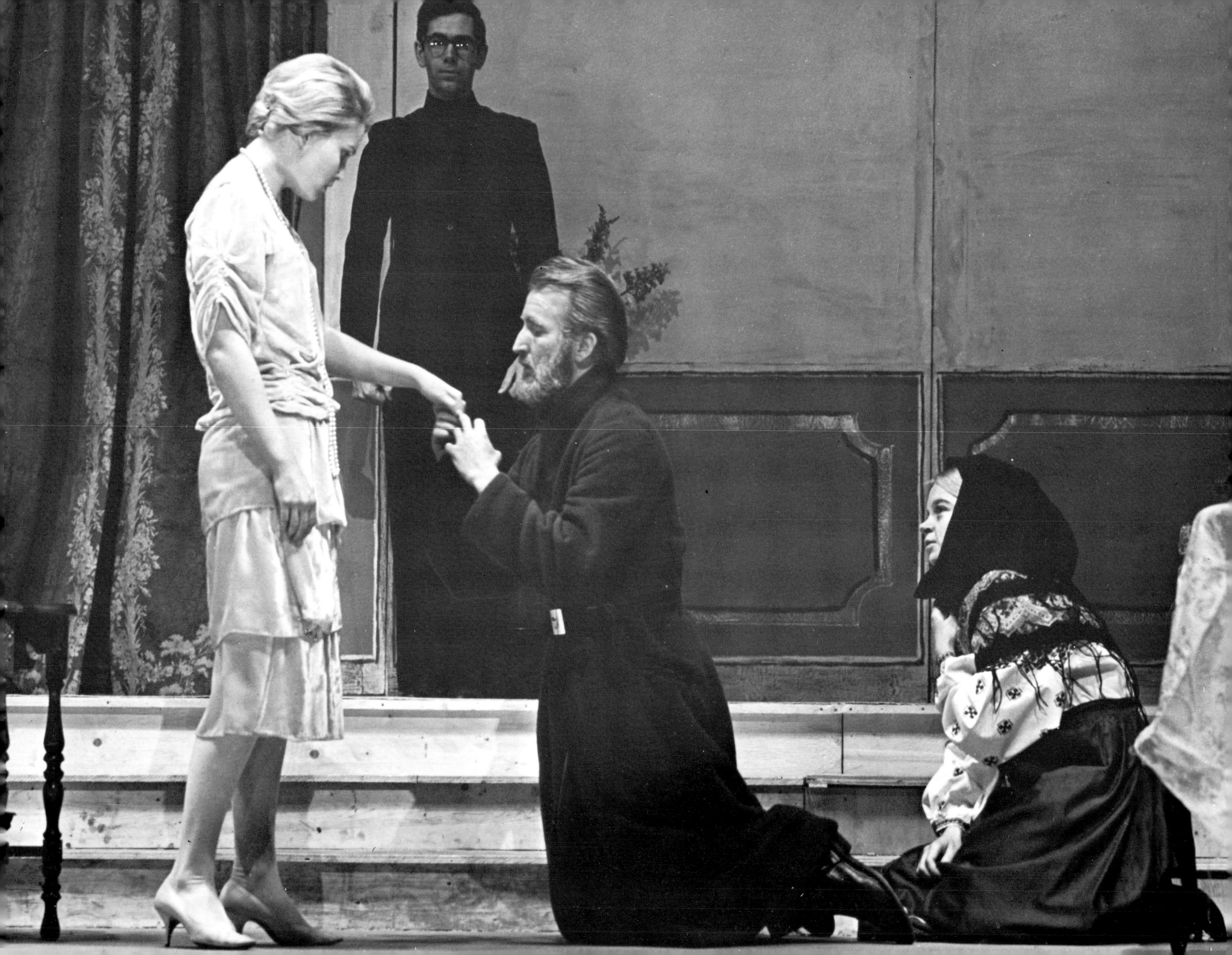

MOONLIGHT MELODRAMA

5-17 *"Anastasia"* (1964) co-directors M. Houghton/D. Miller, Cambrian Players

national television commercials. Nancy Josie began designing with the Cambrians and now designs professionally in Toronto. Joel Kramer, an American who had the lead role in Cambrian's first Shakespearian production *King Lear*, returned to the United States, and toured as the lead in *Fiddler on the Roof*. And Stephen Taylor, Artistic Director of Moonlight Melodrama for several seasons, and a professional actor, also played in *Lear*.

The Cambrian Players are now a nationally known theatre company. They're a hard working group of volunteers who know theatre, and are keenly devoted to maintaining theatrical excellence throughout Thunder Bay, and consistently set the example. We've come to associate them with the Lakehead University theatre, where in all likelihood, they'll continue to present their productions. But wherever they decide to work, and whatever they choose to present, local audiences can look forward to what they've come to expect since 1949 -- the very best in live theatre.

It was in the spring of 1972 that Thunder Bay's first professional theatre company was born. During the previous winter, a group of theatre arts students at Confederation College, discovered that besides learning a lot about theatre, they were having a wonderful time just working together, so even before the course ended, they decided to form a company.

Someone suggested that they approach the shipping companies with the idea of travelling up and down the Great Lakes, doing a sort of show boat, but that idea soon died. For one thing, it would be just too costly, and for another, what shipping company would disrupt its busiest season to accommodate a group of unknown actors?

But part of the idea had been to perform melodramas, so when they scuttled the ship, they at least saved melodrama, and from that basic idea, the company's format evolved.

Bill Pendergrast, their instructor, agreed to direct the troupe, which included Nancy Bates, David Duffield, Kim Hansen, Rene Boyer, Brian Duffield, Glory Jordan, Maureen McEachern, and Joanne Mayotte. Gail Bilborough was also part of the original company, as was Teresa Castonguay, Nino La Bilato, Ralph Gill, Greg Reid, and Joe Saunders. Once the decision was made to form the company, away they went.

"Basically, we committed ourselves to working an entire

5-18   *Moonlight Melodrama's first location on the corner of Pearl and Water Streets*

5-19   *"The Orphan's Locket" (1977), director S. Claydon, Moonlight Melodrama*

5-20   *"Dracula" (1975), director R. Gailbraith, Moonlight Melodrama*

summer with very little money and just doing it," recalls Teresa Castonguay. "And in a way, it was rather funny, because everybody just spread out in a million different directions, and we wandered around town, looking for a suitable old building. Finally, we found the old 'O.K. Rooms' down at Water and Pearl. Totally empty, except for this gorgeous bar -- oak, and full length. It was just beautiful. So we asked the City if we could have it for the summer -- you'll recall that urban renewal was in progress right around there at that time -- and they gave it to us for a dollar.

"That was wonderful, in itself, but then the company had to turn to and get it in order. This meant tearing down walls, partitions, removing the outdated plumbing and heating, and installing washrooms. In the process, the cast learned quite a bit about skills they never knew they had, and a great deal about this quaint old rooming house that had quite a reputation around old Port Arthur. One of the discoveries was that we had inherited a ghost.

"I had an office on the second floor, and one night I was working late up there, and heard footsteps coming along the hall, knocking on doors, and opening and closing doors. I thought it was just one of the company wandering around.

"Eventually, I came downstairs and asked who had been upstairs. And you see, there were problems up there, because we had been told not to go past a certain area, but these footsteps had done a complete circuit of the entire hall. And when everybody denied having gone up there -- which was quite believable, since all of them had been busy rehearsing -- we knew that we had a ghost. After that it made many appearances, to others in the company as well as to me, always just thumping and knocking. And it always stayed on the second floor. It never went farther up, nor came down to the main floor."

That first summer was a lot of hard work, because they had to almost literally tear everything out of the building. They also had to rewire the facility, and most of the wiring passed down through a very dark and dank basement which, considering the presence of the second-floor ghost, wasn't anyone's favourite working area.

"And can you believe it? We did *eight* shows that first

summer! *Dirty Work at the Crossroads, Only an Orphan Girl, The Last Loaf, Egad, What a Cad!* and another four whose titles I've forgotten."

Before each show, specially invited performers would present what were called oleos, designed to warm up the audience. These people sang and sometimes led the audience in singing, and it was an enjoyable prelude to a night of superb entertainment. Between acts, the cast came out to the bar and served allowable refreshments, and right from the opening curtain, these people were professionals.

Moonlight Melodrama, which was the cast's original name for themselves, caught Thunder Bay quite unprepared. It took most of the summer for their reputation to catch fire, but many patrons of those first shows, have come back every year for more.

While they were still operating on Pearl Street, Moonlight acquired another phenomenon besides the ghost. This happened the first time they presented *Dracula*. They picked up a real, live bat. They've done *Dracula* five times and in more than one location, and each time, a live bat has come into the theatre.

"Really spooky," says Teresa. "It happened even out at Chippewa. And in 1979, we did *The Passion of Dracula,* and the bat suddenly appeared in the theatre on opening night."

At Pearl Street, they couldn't get the bat out of the building, so it stayed for the duation, often swooping down over the audience, who thought this was a clever ploy done with finesse. There was also what can only be called the crash of Bat-747.

"With *Dracula*," says Teresa, "there always has to be some kind of bat appearance, and we've constructed them of several types. But this particular one was made of two-by-fours, crossed at right angles. We were at the Pot Pourri Building in the Exhibition Grounds at the time, and Shirley Claydon was on stage as Dr. Van Helsing. This bat was supposed to swoop across the stage, and then take off to the other side. Well, somehow it slipped its moorings and this immense wooden thing flung itself straight down on Shirley, and hit her on the head. She collapsed right there in the mdidle of her performance. So really, bats have been something of a plague to us."

Since it started, Moonlight has moved around fairly often.

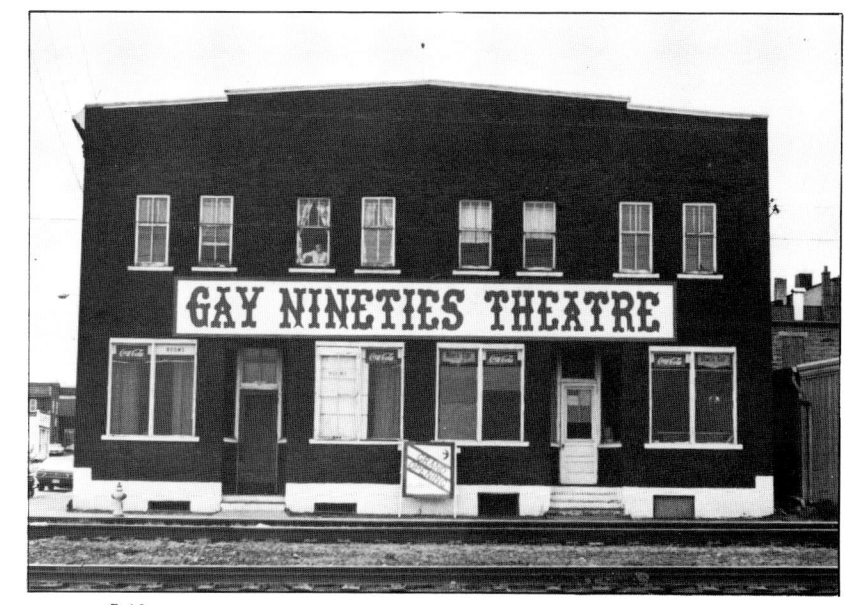

5-18

they were at Pearl Street until 1974, spent a year in the old LaPrade Hotel and would have stayed longer if the building hadn't been ruined by fire during the winter. After that, having lost considerable costumes and scenery, they moved to the Pot Pourri Building at the Exhibition Grounds. After one summer, that was obviously an impossible place logistically, especially during the C.L.E., so they went to Confederation College for a season.

In the summer of 1977, Moonlight went to Sioux Narrows for two weeks, and then did a short run at the Jackpine Community Centre on Oliver Road. That winter, they started looking again for some place to perform, and came up with the old pavilion at Chippewa Park. They played there from 1978 until 1983, then had to move to the Prince Arthur Hotel for the 1984 season, because of repairs to the jack-knife bridge. This year, they returned to Chippewa and had a very successful summer.

"Chippewa's a nice place," says Past-President Sharon Younger. "The only problem is the roof leaks in the dressing rooms, so all the makeup tends to get rained on."

But each of the moves that Moonlight has made, has represented about $10,000 worth of renovations, not counting labour, and it has taken its toll.

"Every year," says Sharon, "the capital that we would have used to mount the production, to make our costumes, our sets and all that, went into just making a theatre. So it's nice to be at Chippewa Park, because all of that has been done. The only problem is that Chippewa isn't easily accessible to people without cars."

Nowadays, Moonlight has a Board of Directors which includes Joe Saunders, one of the original company. Under the guidance of Stephen Taylor, a professional actor who began his career in Thunder Bay, and who is now the Artistic Director, Moonlight presents three plays per season. Each one runs continuously for two weeks and then, after all three have been staged, they run on alternate nights. The theatre opens July 1st, and runs until the Labour Day weekend.

Today, Moonlight is one of very few companies in Canada or the United States, which exclusively presents melodrama, and their productions are done in exactly the same way that touring players presented them in the early days of theatre. Indeed, many of their productions probably were first presented here in the old Port Arthur Town Hall in the 1880s. But new plays also appear regularly at Moonlight. Founding Director Bill Pendergrast wrote *The Secret of the Spyglass* which Moonlight premiered in its first few years. More recently was the local story *Lady Lumberjack*, by local author Gordon McLaughlin.

And so, while Moonlight appreciates the arrangements in the old pavilion at Chippewa Park, they feel that it isn't their final home. They're still looking, knowing that when they do decide to move, it will be an agonizing chore, even though they now have considerable experience at it.

"In a way," says Sharon Younger, "we envy Magnus, because they started at about the same time as we did, but they found their building on McLaughlin Street. Over there, nothing like urban renewal was going on, and so, once they moved in, they could stay. Now, it's really a charming little place, and one that's widely recognized. People know where they are, and think of a specific building when they hear the name. Maybe some day, we'll have that kind of an image, too."

Thunder Bay's popular summer stock company is partly funded by government grants, and receives generous help from the City of Thunder Bay. Although it's a professional company, it's also a venue wherein local amateurs can gain experience, and it's an ideal palce to go during the summer, for excellent, live theatre. The menu is always family, and it's always light. Nobody's sleep has ever been disturbed by something that Moonlight produced, although there have certainly been surprises to more than just the audience.

Especially when they do *Dracula*.

Early in 1970, a letter reached Gordon Dalzell, the newly appointed Director of the Lakehead Board of Education. It came from a chap named Lancaster, somewhere in England, and said something about wanting to start a professional theatre in Thunder Bay. The first name that Mr. Dalzell could think of was Dusty Miller, so he passed the letter on to her.

"He (Burton) picked us," says Dusty, "because we looked to be 'in the centre', and he thought maybe that was a good place to have a theatre. He didn't know anything about us. He'd been in Canada briefly, but

5-20

MAGNUS

5-21

5-21 "Fire" (1985), director B. Richmond, Magnus Theatre

away down east in Prince Edward Island, and he wondered whether anybody could give him any information, and was the community ripe, yet, for a professional theatre? He had just picked names out of a hat, really.

"Well, I thought about it and thought about it and said, 'Well, yeah, I think maybe it is; particularly the kind of theatre where you're prepared to do stuff for children as well as adults. I mean, I can see it working by doing stuff in classrooms and taking special shows out to the schools, and things like that.'

"So my letter went off, and the next thing I knew, I got a phone call from the chap, Burton Lancaster. He'd just flown over, and was looking into possibilities. He didn't think there was any point in coming here, but his wife had phoned him in Montreal or Toronto or wherever he was, and had said, 'Well, we've got this letter from this lady, you know, so why not go up and see her?'

"The next thing I knew was he arrived on my doorstep. This was 1971, and it just so happened that I was involved in a provincial election. We were also getting ready -- Tom and I -- the minute this election was over, to leave Canada and go on sabbatical. So Burton Lancaster arrived, and I said, 'Great I'm glad you're here. I'll do what I can for you, but I have very little time.'

"So I roared him around and introduced him to a number of people, and said, 'You're on your own. You're just going to have to talk to them'."

One of them was Carol Bell, who was the incoming President of Cambrian Players, and the Dramatic Arts teacher at Hillcrest High School.

"What kind of a person would do something like that?" she laughed, repeating my question. "Only Burton Lancaster. Oh, he's a super person. He sort of looked like a funny troll, is my impression of him. He wasn't tall, and was rather round, but dynamic energy and very stubborn. He had to be stubborn."

Carol, who could give him more time than Dusty, under the circumstances, was able to introduce him to people and let him do a lot of talking; enough that when he got back down east, and did a lot of thinking, it wasn't long until he came back.

Oddly enough, when he returned, he stayed at the Royal Edward Hotel, just as two other dreamers had done a little over a decade earlier -- Messrs. Charrier and Dahlgren.

"I seem to remember it was winter when he brought his family," says Carol, "because they didn't know how to cope with this kind of season. And I think, too, that Burton fell that first winter and broke a leg. And he wasn't a small man at all, so I remember that being a problem."

It should also have been an omen, especially to anyone connected with theatre. They're such a superstitious lot, that you can't even wish them good luck. You do it by saying, 'Break a Leg'.

And so, to survive, Mr. Lancaster directed *Oh, What a Lovely War* for the Cambrians, as a professional director. He also went to Fort Frances and directed a production up there, and both of these ventures helped keep the family in money. But throughout that winter, he kept ruminating on how best to put together his theatre.

As Carol recalls, the first thing he did here, on his own, was an evening of Pinter plays at Confederation College, and then he gathered some people around him to talk about the whole idea, and to come to grips with the nitty-gritty.

"I was one of them," she says, "and Bill Potter was involved early. Jeff McKay, who now teaches at PACI was one of the first. Joan and John Flatt, I remember also, just talking about the idea; looking at where we could get money to get started."

As it happened, there was a fair amount of money available through government youth programs, and so he decided to start his company on an Opportunities For Youth Program, and call it Theatre in the Park. This was the summer of 1972.

"He continued with those youth programs even after he moved into the building," says Carol, "because it was touch and go for a year or two, and money was hard to find. He knew there was support for his idea, but to find the resources was difficult. In fact, I know that if it hadn't been for the OFY programs or the LIP grants, that Magnus wouldn't have got off the ground.

... They're such a supersitious lot, that you can't even wish them good luck ...

5-22 *East End's Magnus Theatre after renovations, 1983*

... money was hard to find ...

THE SLOVAK HOME

"But Burton was very good at manipulating those types of programs to get the maximum amounts of money, and that's how we got off the ground, until we found the building. We called ourselves Theatre Northwest, and worked out of the old Foresters' Hall on Simpson Street. It was a small place with a basement."

By the time Dusty Miller got back in 1972, Magnus was struggling to take off, and they had acquired their first LIP Grant. They had also found their present building, known as the Slovak Home; a building that had already made its unique contributions to the culture of Thunder Bay.

According to Mr. Vic Tomcko, the Slovak Home goes back many years. Slovakian immigration into this area began in the 1880s, and the first immigrants came here to stay. A second wave arrived between 1920 and 1932, but these immigrants came with the intention of making money and returning to the homeland.

Thus, because they planned to go back eventually, they felt a strong need to keep their Slovakian customs alive and strong, and so they organized the Slovakian Society, which eventually had a membership of 350. Of these, 75% were single men who provided most of the financial support for the society's activities.

"The main purpose of the organization," says Mr. Tomcko, "was to carry on the Slovakian language, culture, plays and concerts. We had our own orchestras. We had people teaching music and dances. Lots of activity.

"The organization had bought an old hall on the present site, in 1937. Sometime in the 1940s, it was decided to build a bigger hall. So, a fellow named Hedastroski bought the adjacent house, sold the building to the Polish Legion on Simpson Street, and donated the land to our organization."

Construction was begun in 1946, and the hall opened in March or April, 1948. From then until about 1964 or '65, the Slovakian culture was carried on in the hall, and it became known as the Slovakian 'Home'.

"I was overseas when the land was bought," says Mr. Tomcko, "but we eventually had a choir of 130 voices, and I sang in it. And we had an orchestra of 80 children. They played mandolins and violins, and were conducted by a Mr. Otto."

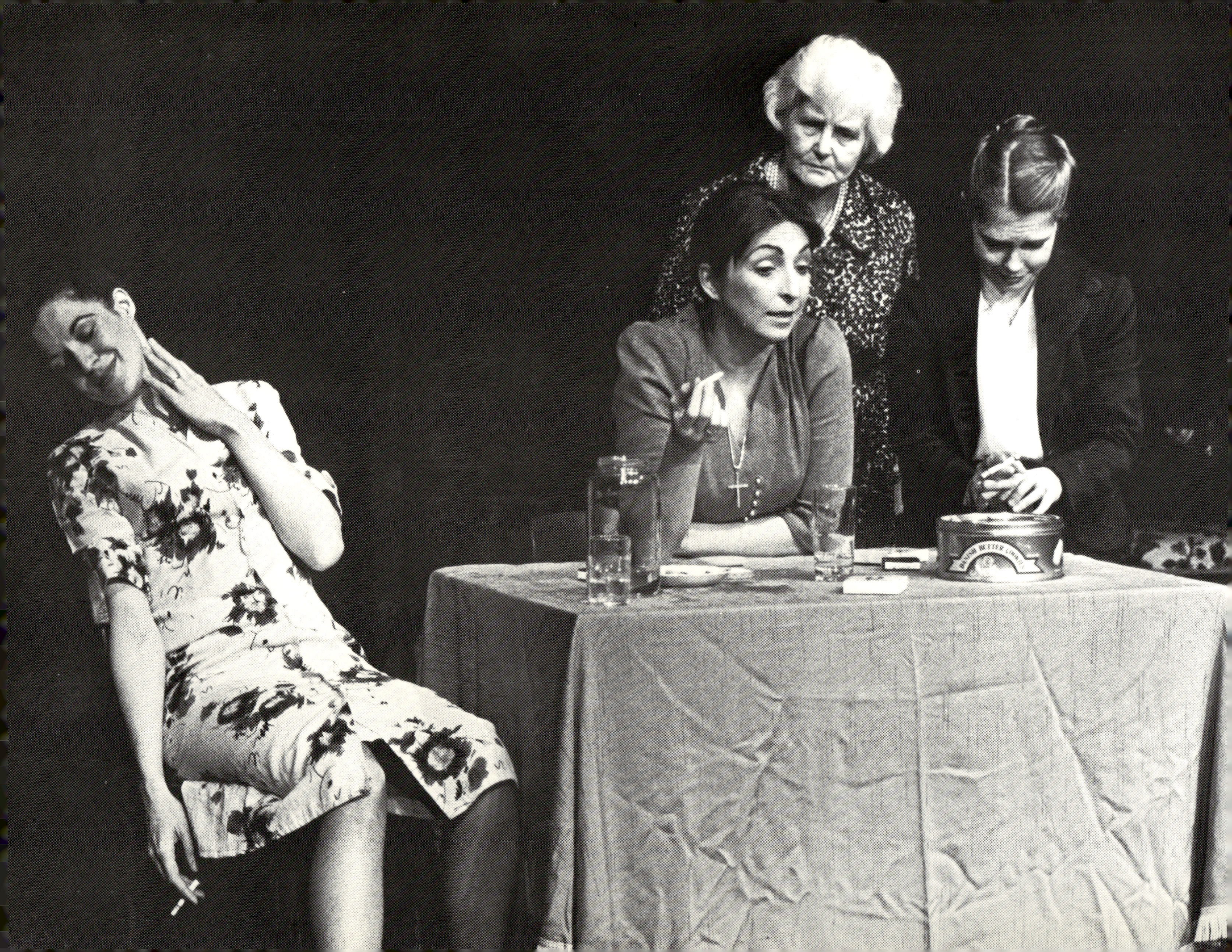

THE RISE OF MAGNUS

... the Cambrians were very, very helpful ...

5-23 *"Waiting for the Parade"* (1981), director T. Feheregyhazi, Magnus Theatre

However, as with so many other people who come to Northwestern Ontario with the intentions of going back where they came from, things didn't work out as planned. Instead of going back home, they stayed, the children grew up and dispersed, and eventually there was hardly anyone left to carry on the culture. By the mid-60s, it was necessary to close the hall, and thus it remained until this man Lancaster came to town.

In 1972, having acquired a grant, Magnus staged its first production: a piece of theatre of the absurd called *The Resounding Tinkle*. Then they hired Dusty Miller.

"That first year," she says, "the Cambrians were very, very helpful. When Magnus got the Slovak Home, I became the first sort of manager. I did everything from cleaning the place, to all the PR, all the box office, all the publicity. And I remember, I did all this for something like $60 a week. And it was incredible. We did a five show season!"

The first one, that opened on January 30th, 1973, was the play *Lion in Winter*. The plot concerns the struggle between Henry II of England and his Wife, Eleanor of Aquitaine as to which of their three sons will become heir to the throne. It had recently been released as a movie, starring Katherine Hepburn.

For the role of Eleanor of Aquitaine, Director Lancaster auditioned 'hundreds of performers' in both Toronto and Thunder Bay, and settled upon Jacqueline McLeod of Port Arthur. Jackie, who was hired in Toronto, had sung here with Roy Coran's orchestra at the Friday and Saturday night dances at the Coliseum back in the 50s. She had spent time singing and acting in Winnipeg, and gone to Toronto as a bookkeeper with the National Ballet Company, before resuming her acting career.

Two local performers who were part of that cast, were Tom Labelle and Teresa Castonguay, both amateurs at the time.

It was at this point that Mr. Peter Faulkner took charge of the children's productions which Magnus had agreed to do. He had come from Atikokan, but had been in Toronto for a few years before coming here. Both his parents had been in theatre, too, and so he had considerable experience to draw upon in mounting the productions that were taken to the schools. It was these projects that did most to keep Magnus afloat during those first couple of

. . . He had been required by the actors' union to change his legitimate name . . .

TIBOR

5-24   *"Hedda Gabler" (1982), director K. Reis, Magnus Theatre*

years. And of course, several other people also deserve credit individually, for personally backing loans at the bank, which paid expenses until grants arrived, only to be reborrowed when the grants were spent.

Of course, although Burton Lancaster could be called a bit of a dreamer in having come here at all, it should also be pointed out that the man wasn't exactly a babe in the woods. He had acted for years in London's East End, and in Canada and the United States. He had been directing for some time before he came here, and had managed at least one ballet company on tour. He had been required by the actors' union to change his legitimate name from Burt Lancaster to Burton, because of a conflict with that other chap -- whom he had met, incidentally, and liked very much.

By 1974, Magnus was rolling. The old seats, on which Carol Bell and her Hillcrest students had so painstakingly sewn cushions that first year, were regularly filling. By 1976, Mr. Lancaster could plainly see that his dream had, in fact, begun to succeed, and so it was time to move on. He handed in his resignation to the Board of Directors, and left that fall, undoubtedly very happy at having done what he came here to do, and surely with a sense of pride at having founded a successful theatre. Thunder Bay was happy, too.

For the 1977/78 season, Magnus hired Mr. Maurice Evans to be resident actor/director while they found Burton's replacement. And if you knew Burton Lancaster, and imagined that he was dynamic, you really should have stuck around and met Tibor Feheregyhazi.

Tibor had been an Hungarian revolutionary in 1956, and fought the Russians in the streets of Budapest. A year before that, he had acquired his Master of Acting degree at the National Theatre School in Budapest. His mother had produced musical shows during the war for Radio Hungary, and his father was a journalist. He himself had been a child actor on Radio Budapest during the final days of World War II, and for a period afterwards, although his main task during the final battles was to bury the dead.

"I was 12 years old during the siege," he told me one day, sitting in his office on Miles Street. "And our apartment was about two blocks away from Radio Budapest, so during the bombardment, if anything had to be done by actors my age, they sent for me and I went and did it. And at the end, we were broadcasting right from the bunker."

After getting his acting degree, Tibor worked in Hungary until the revolution, then went to Italy and worked as an extra in a Selznick film. While there, a friend recommended that he go to Canada, and so he ended up washing hospital floors in Ottawa.

Then there appeared an ad in the paper asking for students to take language lessons, which he misunderstood to be one asking for people to teach foreign languages, but when he phoned the lady, it led to his being introduced to Ottawa's Little Theatre. In it, he directed a young Smiths Falls disc jockey named Rich Little, before moving to the National Theatre School in Montreal. Then he went to Winnipeg's Manitoba Theatre Centre, which was where Burton Lancaster found him. He recalls his reactions:

"Burton Lancaster! Gods! I went to the airport to see him, but he didn't look like Burton Lancaster. He looked like somebody else. And here it was this guy from Thunder Bay that I had loaned costumes to a few years before. His wife and he had come to the MTC wanting to borrow costumes, and I gave them what they needed, but I also showed them Manitoba Theatre Centre, and they had gone back home, and that had been it. And then, two or three years later, here they were back again.

"So he said, 'Look, I'm leaving the theatre. Would you be interested to have a theatre of your own?' And I said, 'Yes, but I have to see it'.

"So I came down here a few times, and saw a few shows, and saw the whole place, and said, 'Yes, I would be interested'."

His first play was *Equus*, in the fall of 1978. And by the time that season ended, he had talked local contractor Tom Jones into renovating the theatre as a donation. Mr. Jones has always supported the performing arts in this city, and he did so again, convincing all his subcontractors that they should do likewise. And so, Magnus was renovated at roughly half of what it should really have cost.

The new Magnus auditorium now holds 194. Tibor had laid out an overall 3-phase plan -- enlarge the auditorium, enlarge the stage, enlarge the theatre. He had accomplished phase one.

In the years between then and 1982, the year Tibor and

5-24

his family moved to Saskatoon, many were the successes. *Hosanna, Cabaret, Waiting for the Parade, Pygmalion, The Three Penny Opera*, and others. More than one, like *Forever Yours Mary Lou*, offended people.

"Lots of people left the theatre because of that one," he said, thoughtfully, the last week he was here, "but it really was a wonderful production. And you know, I met people who I think had that situation right in their own families. We touched a terrible chord in that one, but sometimes, that's our business. We can't just entertain. And I still think that Tremblay is one of our greatest writers."

When Tibor left, it was because he felt he knew his audience too well, and that it would be unwise to stay any longer. "As a director," he often said, "you're only as good as your next opening night. It doesn't matter what you've done in the past."

Brian was the founding Artistic Director of Persephone Theatre in Saskatoon, and has directed more than 50 productions for theatres all across the country. He has mounted all three Canadian productions of *Cruel Tears*, including the national tour seen at Centaur Theatre in Montreal. His production of *The Windigo* for Vancouver's Green Thumb Players toured Europe in 1980. He has also served as Dramaturge for the Playwrights' Workshop and taught at New York State, Simon Fraser, Concordia, McGill, and the National Theatre School in Montreal.

"When I came here," he says, "I felt that I inherited a very rich legacy as a theatre company. On paper, perhaps, it didn't look very rich, but what was so rich about what Tibor and Burton had left me, was the fact that there had been a direct relationship with the audience. You really have a sense, here, of an audience that has been built and is carefully interested in each selection that comes along. And I think our shows pay off that way.

"That doesn't mean that they flock to every one, but they certainly support every show, whether or not they approve of it. And when they like a show, they come out in enormous numbers. This city is very very fast to respond.

"We've done good publicity and bad, but ultimately it's word of mouth in Thunder Bay that really counts. And I think that speaks very highly for Magnus in terms of what Tibor and Burton have done to build that

5-25 *"I Love You, Anne Murray"/ "Love is Strange"* (1984), director B. Richmond, Magnus Theatre

BRIAN RICHMOND

"When I came here, I felt that I inherited a very rich legacy as a theatre company..."

5-25

> *... there's an intimacy with the audience ...*

> *... Variety in New York often writes about the quality of new work being done here ...*

sensibility into the audience. It's a very precious thing."

He also found an established physical theatre, already renovated, and in which the company had lived for over a decade. So, unlike at least one other local company, there was neither need nor desire to move.

"In the 25 years I've been in Canadian theatre," says Brian, "I've witnessed a history of disasters of theatre companies moving from their original location to another one. I think the last thing Tibor said before he left, and I still agree with him, is that the place of Magnus is in the east end of the city.

"There's a charm about the place, and it's historic and there's an intimacy with the audience that gets lost when you move, and that, to us, is our most precious commodity; our relationship with our audience."

But Brian Richmond didn't inherit a theatre company that was without problems. Like his predecessors, he also finds there are just too many people working in the available space. Tibor had been able to extend the auditorium but the stage remained miniscule. In 1983, when Phase Two was completed and the lobby, lower lounge, and stage were enlarged, it eased the problem somewhat, but did not erase it.

"We're now entering into a feasibility study to find out precisely what our longterm building needs are," says Mr. Richmond. "Also, to explore how we might finance these long-term building needs. My recommendation is to expand the theatre to approximately 250 seats. But first, we should gradually expand our playing time from 2½ to four weeks. And I think it would only be at that point that we would want to consider expanding the house.

"Meanwhile, we can also do much by giving Magnus a national or North American stature; one that is unrivalled in excellence anywhere on this continent."

Rather excitedly, he points out that this has already begun. *The Financial Times* has referred to our company as one of the most aggressive small theatres in North America. *Variety* in New York often writes about the quality of new work being done here in Thunder Bay. And also, the company completed, in June 1985, its first national tour: *Now Love is Strange*.

"Rehearsals began in Montreal in December," says Brian. "We opened in Montreal's Centaur Theatre, which is the big English Language theatre there. Then we moved to the Arts Club Theatre in Vancouver, then to the Alberta Theatre Projects in Calgary. Then we came home to Thunder Bay, and sold out entirely here, then moved to the Tarragon in Toronto, and finished in June. It was quite prestigious for Magnus."

While that tour was in progress, of course, the regular season continued in Thunder Bay. Moreover, the company co-produced *Gone the Burning Sun* with Centaur in Montreal.

"None of this gives the people in Thunder Bay any direct access to those ideas," he says, "but it does spread our reputation as a theatre company to other cities. This helps us with things like fund raising at the corporate level, which has been a major problem for Magnus, and which will be an even bigger one now that the Auditorium has opened.

"But it helps us, too, just in terms of what our local audiences see, because our productions do have something to do with our reputation. It allows us to have a level and quality of actor that we've never been able to have before in this city. Obviously we can't pay a lot of money, being a small company. But actors don't just work for money. They also want to work for theatres whose quality is good. We can't compete with the big cities monetarily, so we must compete in quality."

In terms of national theatre tours, Mr. Richmond sees them as a once-every-three-years type of thing. For the immediate future, he's much more interested in taking his shows to smaller communities in northern Ontario. He sees Magnus very much as a northern Ontario touring company, or as a northern Ontario company, not just a Thunder Bay company. But one, nevertheless, whose main objective will always be satisfying the Thunder Bay audience at all levels, and getting the sort of feed-back that they've grown accustomed to hearing.

"The things we're most proud of," he says, "are things like when the florist down on Simpson Street goes crazy over *The Tempest*, or knowing that every taxi driver knows about Magnus, and gets to know the actors who come here. And the business people who we meet on a day-to-day level; the drycleaners, or whatever, who really talk about Magnus as though it is something that's here and comes from here; that Magnus is somehow theirs, very personally."

... he's much more interested in taking his shows to smaller communities in northern Ontario ...

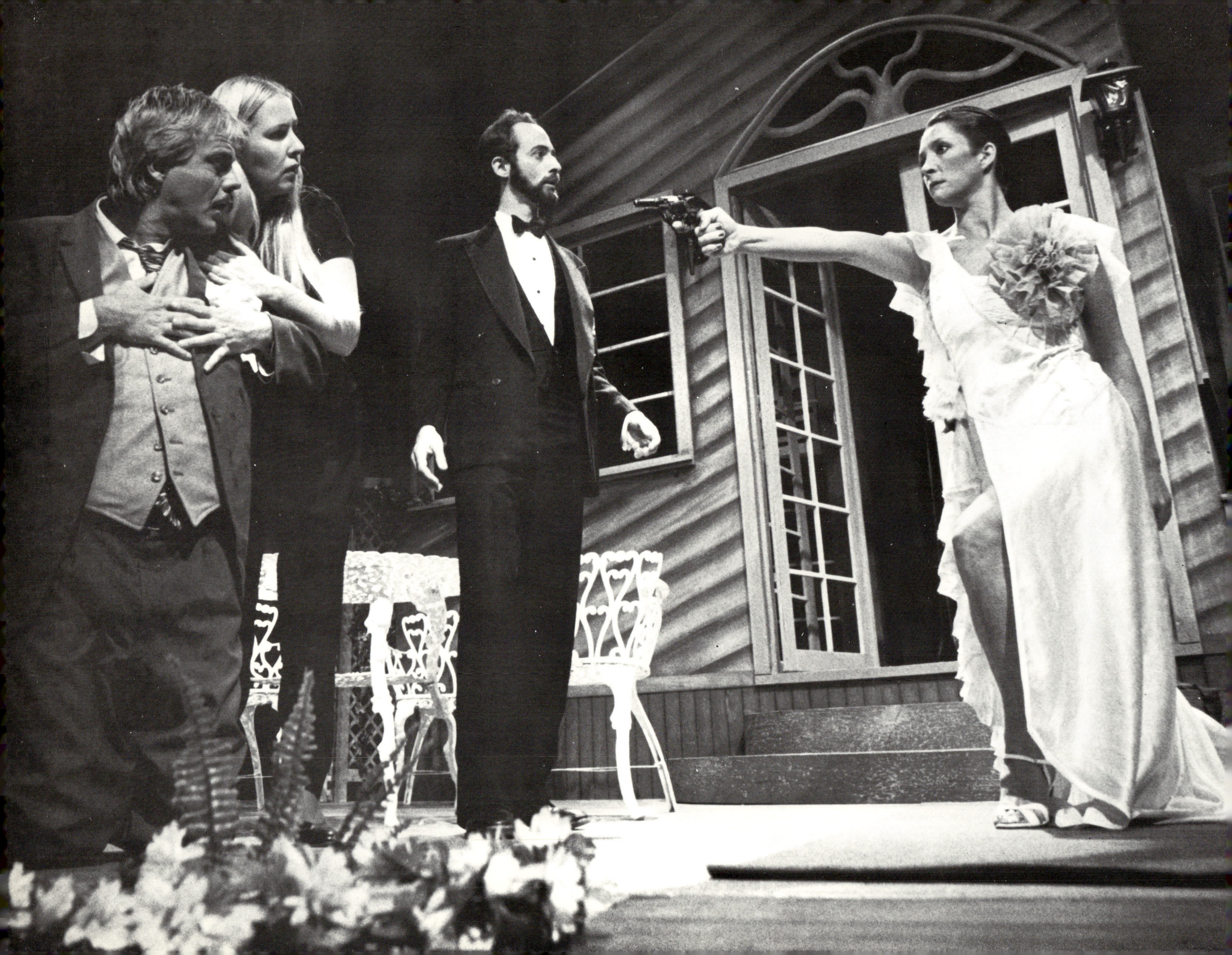

KAM THEATRE

5-26 *"The Art of War" (1984), director M. McKeon, Kam Theatre*

. . . They've been into just about every community in Northwestern Ontario at least half a dozen times . . .

Back in 1974, three young men found themselves out of work in Thunder Bay. That in itself wasn't unusual, but these three had theatre backgrounds. And so, very much as Lakehead people have always done, John Brooks, William Roberts, and Michael Sobota concluded that if their situation was to be improved, they'd have to do it themselves.

They felt that Magnus Theatre was succeeding as a main stream theatre by then, but they wanted to experiment with Canadian plays; something which, at that time, was rather radical.

"We performed one commedia del'arte production outdoors at one of the very early Summer Solstice Festivals," says co-director Michael Sobota. "It was held at a religious ashram on Mokomon Road southwest of Kakabeka Falls, and we received such very happy response to this outdoor comedy, that we decided to try making it an ongoing effort. We were green and naive, of course, but we did some grants applications, contacted other cities and towns, and generally got organized."

In forming what came to be known as Kam Theatre Laboratories, the trio had three purposes. They wanted to find work, to do Canadian plays, and to tour with them.

"We wanted to stay here in Thunder Bay," says Michael, "and work in theatre. Normally, to do that, one gravitated towards bigger cities. We wanted to go to the small towns, and nobody at that time was taking theatre around the region."

In all, Kam Thatre has now mounted over 60 plays, most of which they've taken somewhere. They've been into just about every community in Northwestern Ontario at least half a dozen times. They've visited seven towns in Manitoba, three in Prince Edward Island, three in New Brunswick, two in Nova Scotia, and St. John's, Newfoundland.

"But we probably know Northwestern Ontario as well as politicians do when they travel their ridings," says Michael. "And the response we get in those small towns has been consistently favourable because, you see, nobody goes out to them. So when we drop in, we're often the only thing they see. Many times, we're the first professional live theatre that has ever come to them, and some of these places don't even have movie theatres anymore. So apart from television, they have nothing."

The company is now recognized as one that does Canadian plays, commissions original scripts, and builds collective creations. They've used mime, music, dance, circus skills and masks in their work, woven together in what might loosely be called popular entertainment in the same way that commedia del'arte and melodrama used to be considered popular entertainment, and they've featured those styles of theatre as well as more traditional plays.

Kam Theatre, therefore, is still very much a laboratory although it doesn't call itself that anymore. But it is always experimenting, and is particularly committed to developing local artists. It also has an ongoing program to commission and develop scripts from local writers and composers.

But Kam has never forgotten that it is also a business. It is incorporated as a registered charity, and has a Board of Directors.

"We have a core group of three," says Mr. Sobota. "We call ourselves co-directors, because we're all equal and do the managing and make the artistic decisions. But we also have an associate staff of four, so we're now a full-time company of seven."

Moreover, as each new production comes along, more personnel are contracted on a per-show basis, and so, throughout the year, Kam employs upwards of 60 people.

At least one production per year is taken out of Thunder Bay, and although Northwestern Ontario is their prime area, they haven't been afraid to try other regions and even other provinces.

"As early as 1978", says Michael, "we went to Toronto, and were the first company from this area to have two plays performed there. We were there for two weeks. One play was about Kaministikwia, and the other about Elliott Lake. Three years later, in the spring of 1980, we launched what was then the first major national tour, and went from Manitoba to St. John's, Newfoundland. And for a small troupe like us, that involved a tremendous amount of organizing. We're very proud of having done it."

The Toronto debut happened by invitation. The Mime Company Unlimited had some available theatre space, the two companies knew each other, and so Kam toured a play through northern Ontario, and finished up in Toronto for two weeks.

5-27

"It had taken us about two months," says Mr. Sobota, "and by the time we got there and set up, everybody was depressed. The theatre was on Danforth Avenue, a three-floor walk-up to get into the theatre space with all our stuff. And when we talked about it, we realized we were all homesick."

Just before the performance, a telegram arrived. It was from Tom and Dusty Miller, wishing us well on our first foray out of the region, and it perked everybody up. It was a link backwards. Somebody knew we were going to be there, and had bothered to send us good wishes."

That made it easier for the company to accept the small attendances they drew. After all, they were in a very large theatre pool, and had no advertising budget. But they liked their audiences, and the audiences enjoyed their work.

Like all the other theatre companies now working in Thunder Bay, the beginning years were tough ones. In fact, at first, Kam had no home. They actually began in a basement apartment on Wilson Street.

"Fred Jones, one of the announcers at CBQ, let us use his aparment," says Michael, "and we rehearsed outdoors in Wilson Park across the street. That's where our first performance was put together."

From Fred's apartment, they moved to an old store on Pacific Avenue, called the Minnesota Confectionary. It had been closed for years, and so they moved in, tore everything out, and built a rehearsal hall and living quarters for three.

From there, they worked at the university's Agora, and then at the studio theatre in Confederation College. When they began creating plays that they wanted to take on tour, they used a network of community halls, ending up at the Ukrainian Labour Temple on Ogden Street, in which they now stage most of their productions.

"At that time, too," says Michael, "we began making the circuit of the rural communities. We'd perform at the Conmee hall, the South Gillies hall, the Stanley Hotel, and places like that. We called them run-outs, because we could go out and come back the same day."

Eventually, they moved farther afield until they've now travelled half way across Canada.

5-28

... We called them run-outs, because we could go out and come back the same day."

5-27 *"A Letter to My Son" (1983), director B. Inksetter, Kam Theatre*

5-28 *"Family Portrait" (1985), director J. Selman, Kam Theatre*

... Nobody knows its real impact yet, but things are going to change, and change very fast."

... all of its work reflects social and cultural concerns ...

Today, they're housed in the old Franklin Street School, which they're studying in terms of opening a performance space right there. Thus, instead of getting bigger, they actually plan to get a little smaller. They have definite plans, however, for a small theatre in another building, which they would like to find in the city's north end; one they could move into and renovate, and keep.

Thus, Kam Theatre is another local group that doesn't plan to use the Auditorium themselves, although sponsoring some other group to perform there, is a distinct possibility.

"Personally, I'm glad the Auditorium has arrived," says Michael. "I want to see other national companies coming through, and performing in decent facilities. I like seeing dance companies, and until this Auditorium opened, we had nothing here for dance. But this Auditorium will certainly change our cultural life dramatically. Nobody knows its real impact yet, but things are going to change, and change very fast."

Even so, Michael Sobota doesn't sound worried. He and his associates have built their company very well, they perform quality work, and they're not afraid to experiment.

"We like to be considered an alternative that you can go to on the spur of the moment," he says. "You don't need to come to us because you've bought a subscription and feel that you have to go. We want to think that each show is going to be interesting enough that you'll go to it, so that we aren't hiding something risky in a subscription series, knowing that you'll go because you already have a ticket."

But you should realize, before you ever go to a Kam production, that you may see something political. The company believes that theatre works to effect social change. It is also entertaining, educational, nourishing and integral to a healthy, diverse community culture. Therefore, all of its work reflects social and cultural concerns, relative to this region, and to the degree of its own limitations.

Its artistic direction and administration, however, is a collective function of the company members, answerable to the Board of Directors. The work is supported by the Canada Council, the Ontario Arts Council, the City of Thunder Bay, corporate and business contributions, private donations and performance revenues.

And Kam Theatre is proud to say that it operates without a deficit.

Not only has Thunder Bay produced great actors and performers, but it has also produced at least one movie. It happened back in 1929, when the Port Arthur Amateur Film Society decided to make its first (and last) film -- *A Race for Ties*.

The story centred upon Dorothea Mitchell, a local pioneer who lived at Silver Mountain and operated her own sawmill. (The same heroine was in a Moonlight Melodrama play entitled *Lady Lumberjack*, written by Thunder Bay writer Gordon McLaughlin, and premiered in 1984.)

The film was the project of a chap named Fred Cooper. He was born in England, and emigrated with his family to Canada when he was 17. His father had been corresponding with Fort William Mayor Joshua Dyke, and he had convinced them of the potential at the Lakehead.

After the family settled here, Fred eventually moved to Port Arthur and established Cooper Bakery Ltd. He also went into partnership with George McComber, to open a movie theatre, and was thus introduced to show business.

But Fred wasn't content just to be on the showing side. He wanted a real piece of the action, and soon bought a camera and began taking his own movies. Remember, this was in 1929.

Eventually, he approached an accountant working for the same bakery, and suggested that they make a movie together. The accountant was Dorothea Mitchell, who had been the pioneer on the old PD&W. Obviously, she must have told him something of her life story, which led to the creation of the scenario called *A Race for Ties*.

The President of the Port Arthur Amateur Film Society was a chap named George Lovelady. It didn't take them long to make the movie, and its first showing took place in Port Arthur's Lyceum Theatre in 1929. The second showing didn't happen until 1970, at which time Miss Mitchell came back to the city from her home in Victoria. Her film was shown at the Odeon Court, followed by a civic dinner at the Prince Arthur Hotel.

In case you'd like to re-run it, there's a copy on file in the

MOVIES MADE HERE

5-29 "A Race for Ties" is screened at the Lyceum Theatre (Odeon Court, 1970) T.B.Mus.

5-29

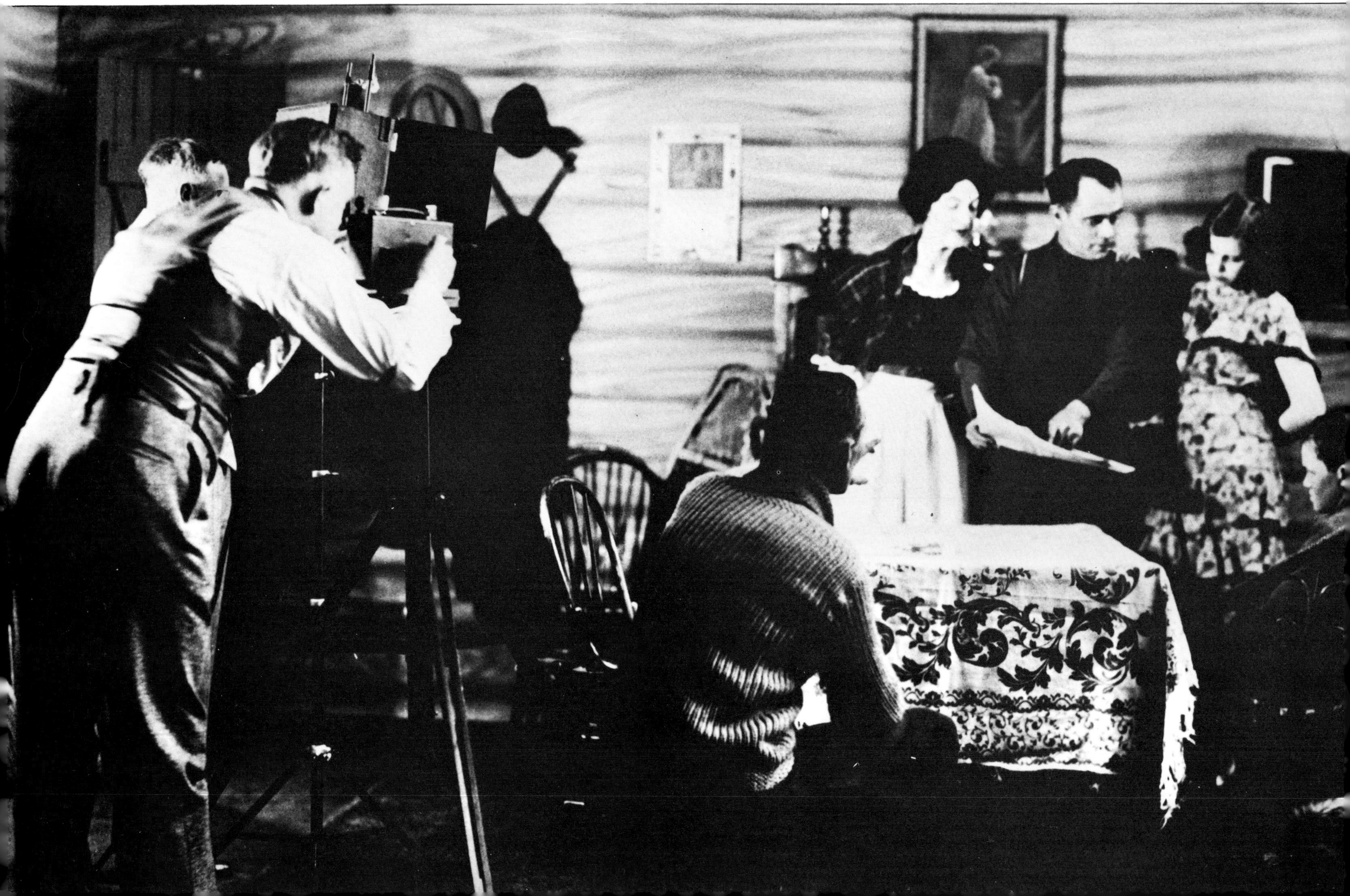

local National Film Board office.

Mr. Cooper's movie wasn't the first ever shot here. When the Noronic was launched at Port Arthur Shipyards on June 2nd, 1913, Messrs. Ross and Murray, the managers of the Royal Theatre, convinced the Pathe studios of Montreal to come up and record the launching. The same ship was filmed at least once more, on September 17th, 1949, when she burned at her pier in Toronto harbour.

Thunder Bay has also hosted at least two world premieres of movies made elsewhere. On Monday, May 3rd, 1943, a National Film Board feature involving H.M.C.S. Port Arthur was shown at the Colonial Theatre, and on Monday, November 4th, 1963, Sheila Burnford's *The Incredible Journey* was given its first showing simultaneously at the Odeon and Paramount theatres in Port Arthur.

For a time, we also had a naturalist and wild life photographer named Ken Campbell living here. In his career, he produced something over 200 documentary films for several organizations. While he was here, he served as the Audio-Visual Coordinator for the Lakehead Board of Education. He and his wife moved to B.C. about five years ago. Mr. Campbell died early in 1985.

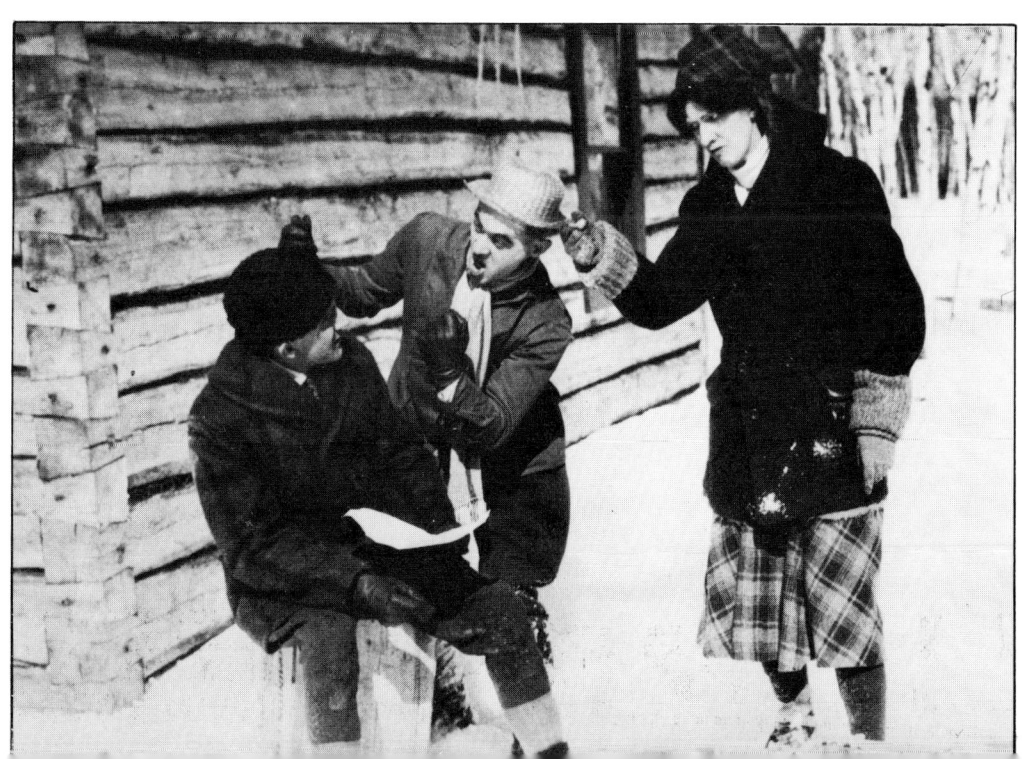

5-30 Cameraman F. Cooper under the direction of P. Harcoutt shoots a scene from "A Race for Ties" with D. Mitchell, Dr. Saunders. M. Lake and E. Cooke   T.B.Mus.

5-31 On location with E. Lindey, W. McComber and D. Mitchell   T.B.Mus.

5-32 Paul Drombolis welcomes author Dorothea Mitchell for the second showing of "A Race for Ties"   T.B.Mus.

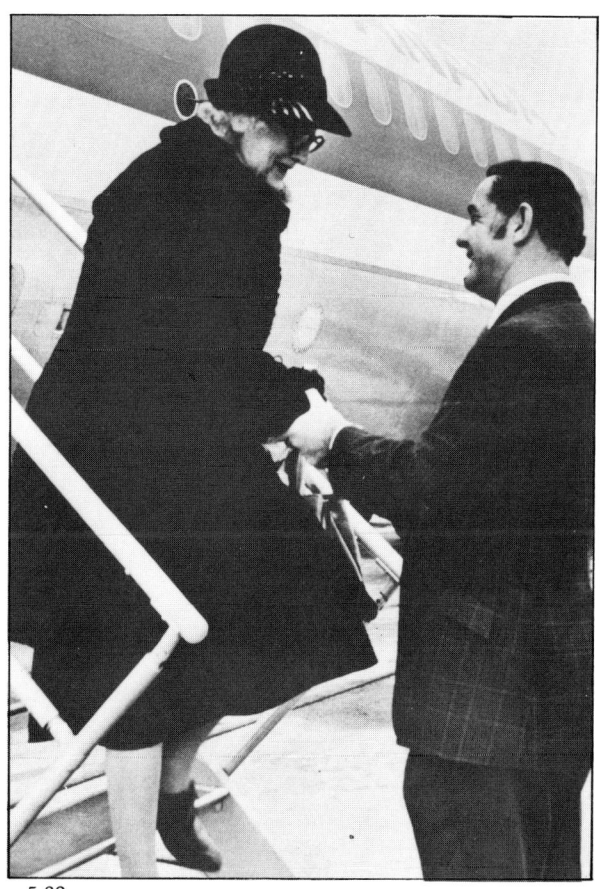

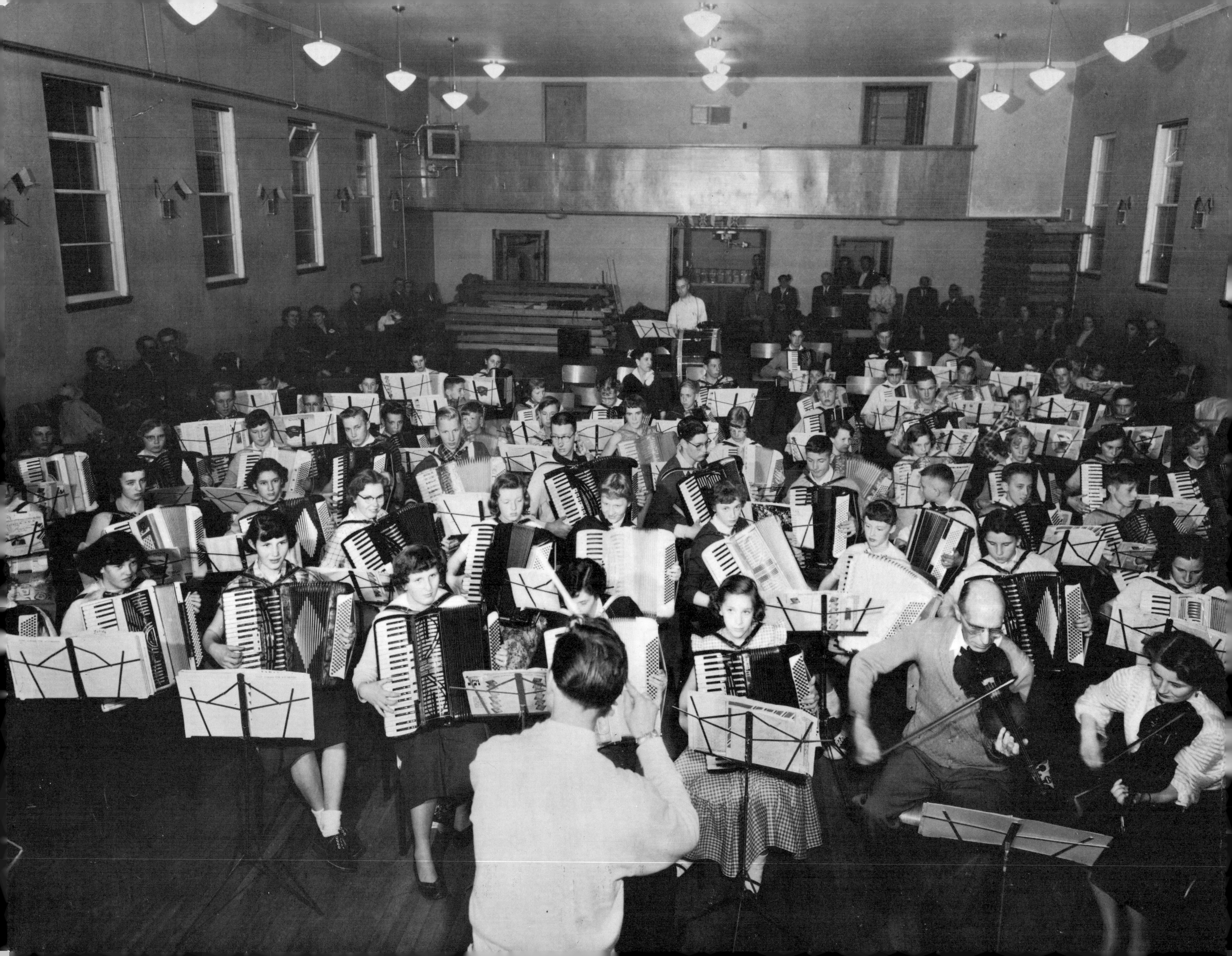

Bands and Musicians

THE MACGILLIVRAY PIPE BAND

6-1 Ralph Colosimo conducting

BECAUSE OF THE NUMBER OF BANDS AND ENSEMBLES THAT FUNCtion in Thunder Bay, it is impossible to give the histories of all. However, here are three whose stories or styles are a little out of the ordinary.

In 1917, the Macgillivray Pipe Band was organized in Fort William. By the 1980s, this band was still functioning and claimed to be the senior private pipe band in Canada, if not in all of North America. It was founded by Dr. Thomas Dow Macgillivray, and although he spelled his name differently, the good doctor was nevertheless related to that other one for whom Old Fort William was originally named.

The band organized at a bad time in the war. Between 1916 and 1918, Canadian forces suffered some of their heaviest casualties. As a result, there was an urgent need for reinforcements. These men were trained in western Canada, sent to the east coast, and shipped overseas as fast as possible.

But in rather typical military fashion, troops passing eastwards through the Lakehead were required to march the five or six miles between the two cities, rather than being allowed to ride the train. And their route lay over a gravel road.

Out of sympathy for the marchers, and enthusiasm for the war effort, a group of local citizens decided to form a pipe band for the purpose of helping the soldiers accomplish their marches. The group came together in the summer of 1917, and Dr. Macgillivray was foremost in finding public support to equip them with instruments and uniforms. Accordingly, he was the first Band Chief, elected the year they formed.

Right from the beginning, the Macgillivrays won high acclaim. Not only were they cheered by the troops whom they voluntarily helped march across the city, but were officially honoured by the Mayor and Council of Port Arthur. They have been prominent in civic ceremonies and parades ever since.

In 1919, they acquired uniforms of the Macgillivray tartan direct from Scotland, and this is the colours they wear today. Branch Number Five of the Royal Canadian Legion quickly made them honorary branch members, and they've been the official band at legion parades and ceremonies for over 60 years.

6-2 *The Ukrainian String Orchestra 1938, with K. Kostyniuk conducting, travelled to district towns like New Liskard and Geraldton, in addition to Toronto performing dances and singing*

THE SENIOR MUSICMAKERS

... the orchestra got its dates mixed up and didn't get there ...

... some have learned the instrument only after retirement ...

Unintentionally, the Macgillivrays also helped spawn three other local pipe bands. In 1922, some original members left the group and formed the Fort William Pipe Band, which later became the Pipes and Drums of Thunder Bay.

Girls' pipe bands also arose in each city, thanks to this split, and excellent training is now available for anyone interested, through the cooperation of the various pipe bands that now function locally.

The Macgillivrays have won awards and acclaim in many places. They've paraded throughout Northwestern Ontario, northern Minnesota, and eastern Manitoba. They've competed more than once at the Canadian National Exhibition's Highland Gatherings in Toronto. They were part of the Massed Pipes and Drums of Thunder Bay in the Rose Bowl Parade at Pasadena in 1972, and were part of the reception for H.M. The Queen at the official opening of Old Fort William in 1973.

Now well past its 65th year, this well disciplined group of musicians rightly ranks among the best pipe bands in the Commonwealth. They work very hard, play magnificently, and their frequent public appearances -- notably at Old Fort William -- consistently demonstrate the outstanding precision for which they are now so widely acclaimed.

And they're Thunder Bay's oldest performing arts group.

One night in 1978, two ladies went to the Herb Carroll Centre, hoping to attend a dance. Somehow, the orchestra got its dates mixed up, and didn't get there so, since one of the girls was a violinist and the other a pianist, they allowed themselves to be coaxed into playing for the dance. That was the start of Thunder Bay's very senior band. The violinist was Eva Giles, a retired violinist from the Thunder Bay Symphony, and the pianist was Mrs. Rose Larrison Stewart, a retired music teacher from New York State.

The band numbers about 15 players, and features violins, guitars and banjos, piano and drums. They're one of the busiest combos in the Lakehead. They hold workshops weekly, rain or shine, winter and summer, and perform at churches, schools, senior citizen's homes, hospitals, festivals and even on the air.

Many members have been playing fiddle most of their lives, but some have learned the instrument only after retirement. Several have

6-2

6-3

6-3 In 1933, the Silvertones were entertaining crowds with 'Big Band' music at the Royal Edward Hotel T.B.Mus.

THE LAKEHEAD MANDOLINS

THE SMITH FAMILY

... Let your fingers do the walking ...

... by the time he was 12, had been crowned National Champion ...

participated in fiddle contest all over the province, and even in Minnesota. A few play in other ensembles.

The Senior Musicmakers produced a recording in 1982, with Lois Garrity as guest soloist. Lois has already made records of her own, besides singing at many local clubs and has appeared on the Tommy Hunter Show.

This is another group that has been playing for a long time. It was organized in 1922, as one of the cultural facets of the Ukrainian Canadian Association. Their music is very European, very warm, and absolutely delightful. They currently number 15 players, and are directed by Mr. Damon Dowbak. They rehearse and perform in the Ukrainian Labour Temple on Ogden Street.

Back in the 1940s, Web and May Smith had a band that played in the CN Hall, which is over by the Jack-Knife bridge. They claimed to be the first combo to use a public address system locally.

Their son Roy learned violin and piano at age six, and was playing guitar, clarinet and saxophone by age eight when he became part of the family band.

As an adult, he was asked to go to southern Ontario, and played with Jack Kane and Mart Kenny. From there he went to New York and appeared with Art Mooney.

During his career, he also did TV commercials, one of which was the jingles and sound mix for 'Let your fingers do the walking through the yellow pages'. He also did audio work at Ontario Place, and performed with Wally Koster.

In 1978, at the age of 44, he was drowned while mooring his sailboat.

Now a young man of 17, Mr. Kris Krienke is an international name in music. He has been heard and seen on television many times, and has recordings to his credit.

Kris learned his banjo from Bob Balabuk, who played with Flipper Flanagan (Jamie Gerow). He attended local schools, finishing high school at Sir Winston Churchill CVI, and by the time he was 12, had been crowned National Champion in his class at the Canadian National Open Banjo

6-4

6-5

6-6

102

6-7

Competition. Other championships quickly followed, and the music has just kept on getting better.

Local 591 of the American Federation of Musicians has 500 members in Thunder Bay, over 100 of whom are full-time musicians. Collectively, they represent a tremendous encyclopedia of musical experiences, and while no attempt could be made to assemble even a representative sample, here are some reminiscences that came up during the interviews for this book:

"In the early days, I played with the City Band, and we had a concert at Chippewa Park every Sunday. Our bandshell was in the lake. About half-way down the lagoon, there was a walk that went out over the water for about 50 yards, and ended at the bandshell.

"That looked very nice, but everything depended on the wind. It blew so hard we had to anchor everything down. And if the wind came off shore, we were nice and comfortable, but nobody heard the concert. If it blew off the lake, they heard every sound but we all froze to death.

"A great place for flowers, but not for bands."

"We played for games in the old Prince of Wales Rink, when there was no heat in it. And it was funny, because whenever we did, all kinds of people would bring a horn in a case. They were in the band, see, so they'd get in for nothing. Then, they'd never come near the band.

"Then one time, the manager asked me how many I had in the band, and I told him 30. 'Well,' he says, 'we've had over 100 people come in here with instruments, who claim they're in the band'."

"It was just amazing, playing a country club job with a piano, a bass, and a drum, and you're the tenor sax player. Then, all of a sudden the booking agent says you're the leader, and the musicians haven't told you who they've played with. You soon find out that they're fabulous musicians, and when you sit down at the end and have a drink, you discover that this guy played with Les Brown, that one with Tommy Dorsey."

"I met Ziggy Elman one time, playing at a banquet. And I said, 'You're Ziggy Elman???' And he said, 'Yes, I am.' And I said, 'What are you doing playing at a banquet?' And he says, 'There's nothing left to play except banquets'.

RECOLLECTIONS

SAVILLE SHUTTLEWORTH

6-4 *Smalltown boy Bobby Curtola makes it in Las Vegas*

6-5 *Country and western music man Tex Leon, 1972*

6-6 *International star Leona Boyd, 1980, St. Paul's United Church*

6-7 *M. Yasenik, W. Zaroski, H. Siczkar, J. Deleo, G. Chernosky at the Flamingo Club playing polka and mixed dance band music, 1959*

ROY CORAN

6-8 *Flipper Flanagan, 1978*

6-9 *The sophisticated sounds of Occasional Jazz included S. Holowitz, B. Simmons, W. Heibein, W. Ulakovic with Bernadette Krouse, vocals*

6-8

6-9

BUD MARTIN

6-10 *Vesnyanka Ukrainian Bandura Ensemble at Ontario Place, 1985 with L. Klymenko, N. Kosoris, M. Obljubek, L. Kozyra, Y Karpiuk*

"I said to him, 'I hold you in awe'. And he says, 'Don't hold me in awe. I'm just a musician, you know. I was just lucky enough that I got on records'."

"In California, I found out that one had better learn how to play the flute, because nowadays, you have to play saxophone, clarinet and flute or you won't get hired. So I took lessons from a guy named Art Smith, who did all the work for Universal Studios, and whatever other studios were left."

"One day he asked me if I'd like to play in the Rose Bowl parade. I said, 'My God!! Do you realize that my mother would willingly go out and kill to have me do that?'

"And he says, 'If you want to play it, just say yes.' So I said YES, and I got a call from the band leader telling me to appear at the Elk's Club at a specified time for rehearsal. We played two marches. That's all we played. The Top Hatters band. It's in the parade every year!

"And what an experience! Coming from this part of the continent and walking down Colorado Boulevard at 85°. You just can't believe it.

"We (The Lakehead Symphony) had the opportunity to bring in the Toronto Symphony Orchestra, and I remember so well, because it was a Board of Directors' meeting in the Prince Arthur Hotel. We didn't know whether we could risk it or not. I think we had to pay them a couple of thousand dollars. And we didn't know whether we could risk that much money because the Winnipeg Symphony had been down a number of times and the sponsors had lost money.

"I remember, finally, Hubert Badanai's daughter was going to the meeting, and she asked what we were all looking so serious about. We told her what we were discussing, and she told us to go ahead and do it, so we all decided to bring in the TSO in the fall. We put it on in the Fort William Gardens.

"Well, the day they flew in, there was a fog covering the airport, and the plane from the east came down over the runway, and we could barely see it 100 feet off the ground. So it took off into the west, and we could just see the dollar bills flying away with it. We had Saul Laskin down there to meet them.

"And we thought, 'Holy Cow! What are we going to do now?? We're going to have to tell these people that there's no concert.' But the plane went off into the west, circled around for awhile, and in an hour or so, the fog burned off and they landed. And it was a very successful project. Just about a packed house."

7-1

Rock and Roll

Rock and Roll

PAUL SHAFFER

. . . she encouraged me to play by ear . . .

7-1 Paul Shaffer, 1966

. . . they'd just cruise around in a great big circle . . .

THANKS TO NATIONAL TELEVISION, AND ESPECIALLY TO DAVID Letterman, the name of Paul Shaffer is something of a household word these days. Paul has been Mr. Letterman's band leader for over three years, and has been making music most of his life. He says he got started here in Thunder Bay -- or Fort William, as his part of the city was called in those days.

"I started when my parents forced me to take piano lessons, like all good parents do," he says. "I had two very wonderful teachers, Mrs. Helen Hardy and Mr. Nelligan. What was so remarkable about Mrs. Hardy was that she encouraged me to play by ear. Most classical piano teachers discourage that. They feel that if a kid learns to play by ear, he'll always fake it, and won't really learn how to read music."

Mr. Shaffer admits that this is exactly what happened in his case. Mrs. Hardy would play the lesson for him, and he'd pick it up by ear. So, although he didn't learn how to read music very well at the time, he did develop the ability to play by ear, and claims that he now makes his living by doing just that.

Most important to his training was when rock and roll came here on radio about 1960. The new style fascinated him. He listened to it very carefully, started learning it, and has kept it up ever since.

"We had a band here", he recalls, "a rock-and-roll band. Bob Anuik was the singer, Ian Rosser on bass guitar, Rick Lazar, and at various times, other members. A guy named Don Murray, another named Frank Dimichelle, and Peter Demion. But we ended up just as a four-piece.

"We played at high school dances; FWCI, Westgate, the Port Arthur schools, all of them. And we would have a regular engagement Saturday nights at the Fort William Gardens. This would be about 1966."

In those days, the Gardens laid plywood on the ice, and the idea was that you danced on the wooden surface, with the band up on stage. But as Paul discovered, most of the people didn't dance.

"Mainly, they'd just cruise around in a great big circle," he recalls. "They'd walk around the outside of the floor. Maybe there'd be a couple of people dancing, and then a whole bunch of people just walking around. And for us, looking down on all this from the stage, was really funny. It looked like kind of a big slushy thing, just moving around."

... They never applauded ...

THE BIG BREAK

... he played all sorts of jobs ...

The musicians took their muic very seriously. They rehearsed all the time, learning the newest songs as soon as they hit the air. They even got advance tapes from the radio stations and learned medleys of songs.

"We did choreography; little shows," he says, "and we'd play these things. We'd finish a 10-minute medley of all our favourite songs with the cleverest transitions we could possibly think of. There'd be silence!

"Nobody would clap, you know. It was really, really tough, but I guess it was pretty good training. Certainly it was the toughest audience I ever had. They never applauded. But you know, good training to play for an audience like that.

"And we'd really work hard, trying to get them to pay attention to us. Of course, they never did. But we used to come up with a lot of performance tricks. Any of them that I pull out to this day, and use in the bands I put together, they always work; the stuff I developed right here. Although, nowadays, people seem to pay attention more."

After graduating from Fort William Collegiate, Mr. Shaffer took sociology and philosophy at the University of Toronto. He had decided to give up music and be an academic. Except that in the third year, he discovered he wasn't happy and started playing in a jazz combo around the city, quickly realizing that this was what he really wanted to do.

"So, in the summers, I'd come back here," he recalls, "and instead of getting a summer job, I'd play in lounges around town. I played a little solo piano at the Circle Inn for a couple of summers. I had a little cocktail trio for dancing, too, and played more rock-and-roll stuff at the other rock clubs and lounges around town.

"Same thing, though. No applause. I don't know where this tradition started, but it certainly toughens you up for later. It makes it that you can really stand anything, after playing to these crowds here."

After graduating from university, Mr. Shaffer decided to take a year to see if he could get work in the music business. If it didn't work out, he was prepared to go to graduate school or into law. So he played all sorts of jobs around Toronto; fashion shows, bars, weddings, and still playing with his original little jazz combo. He felt he was widening his horizons and

... I played Saturday Night Live for five years ...

7-2 Paul Shaffer in session with D. Hurdon, vocals, and R. Lazar on drums, 1966

learning a lot about jazz, at least the kind his group was playing.

"At the end of that year, I got a lucky break," he says. "A Toronto company was being put together of an off-Broadway show *Godspell*. I accompanied a few of my friends who auditioned for roles in it, and ended up getting hired as band leader.

"The composer, Stephen Schwartz, came up from New York for the final auditions, happened to like the way I played, and hired me on the spot that day. He told me to put together a band, and I became the Musical Director of the Toronto company of *Godspell*, at the Royal Alex."

It was his first professional show business experience. He played in it for a little over a year, as it left the Royal Alex and moved into the smaller theatres that make up what's called the Bayview Playhouse. The show was very successful.

"Then Stephen Schwartz took me to New York for the first time, to use me on the sound track of the movie, *Godspell*," he says. "About a year later, I moved to New York to work for him again in the Magic Show on Broadway, where I was Assistant Conductor and pianist in the pit."

He played that show for a year also, and then was hired by the people who started the Saturday Night Live TV show. They knew he was there, and their band leader, Mr. Howard Shore, asked him to come and play piano.

"So there I was on national TV, playing piano," he says. "And I played Saturday Night Live for five years, during which time I was promoted from pianist to writer of special musical material, and even a supporting actor on the show. All the while, building up my reputation in the studio scene in New York; doing studio work, playing on recordings and commercials, and things like that."

When he left Saturday Night Live, Paul free-lanced for a couple of years as a studio musician and arranger, and then got a call from David Letterman, who hired him as his band leader. He has been with the show for over three years, and obviously enjoys being there.

He says that he learned to write music from his two music teachers back in Thunder Bay, in the Royal Conservatory of Music theory and harmony courses. Also, one year, instead of coming home for the summer, he

THE EVOLUTION OF ROCK AND ROLL

7-3 Local 1970s rock band NRG
poster

7-4 Mike Coghlan of Everybody's
Children, 1966

. . . It was really black music, just made a little more 'palatable' for white audiences . . .

7-3

took an arranging course.

"But really, you learn mainly from doing it in a pressurized situation," he says. "I had the rudiments, but the first time I got a job in New York to arrange a record, I stayed up all night and worried over it."

According to Paul Shaffer, a lot of the early rock-and-roll bordered on swing. It was big band music, that was really swing and blues combined.

"Black music," he says. "They used to call it race music at the time. Swing; black gospel music, and hillbilly music combined. And this thing called rock-and-roll started from that. It was originally only for black people. White people would never get to hear these records. Like, they were called race records. They weren't really 'fit' for white ears at that time. Then Elvis Presley, who was a southern kid; a country guy, a rock-a-billy kind of guy, started having hits with his versions of some of these black records, and that started to make the pieces heard by white audiences.

"Then there was a disc jockey named Allan Freed, who used to play a lot of the black records. He's credited with coining the term 'rock-and-roll'. It was really black music, just made a little more 'palatable' for white audiences."

To Paul Shaffer, the early rock-and-roll was the most exciting because it was seminal, or close to the source. It was, he says, just one step removed from the original black music.

"It was innovative and it hasn't really changed much," he says. "I think it has really just become inbred now. When I was a kid, my early influences were Elvis Presley and Gene McDaniels, and all of these early rock and roll artists. And then, of course, the Beatles, who were really just taking what they learned about American black music, taking it over to England and sending it back to us.

"Nowadays, kids grow up and their influences are Led Zepplin, and the 70s rock-and-roll acts, who were influenced, themselves, by the black music. So now, it's like three or four steps removed, and it's all influenced by all of them. But I'm still very loyal to the music that was current when I was a kid, and I don't think it's just because I'm a nostalgist. I think it's because it really was the most exciting then. That's when all the innovations happened."

He says there are now people who do experimental music, and combine rock-and-roll with all kinds of other music.

"It all comes out a crazy kind of mish mash," he says, "but the music that still moves you is that steady four/four beat, and it always will."

When asked why people insist on playing rock music as loud as possible, he was thoughtful.

"I think part of it is that kids have to have their own music, that their parents just don't understand," he laughed. "It's just part of the fun of growing up. You have to. I did my share of listening to loud music when I was growing up, and so did everyone else. You just have to alienate your parents. It's part of what growing up is all about. Also, kids have an affinity to be able to really absorb themselves in music. We lose that as we grow up, because worries about the everyday world take over. But kids don't have worries about the everyday world.

"In my room when I was 15, I used to absorb myself right into a record; really get right into it so that everything else disappeared. And part of it is that you just want to turn it up so loud that everything else disappears, and you're held there in the middle of all that music. You just want to be right there at the centre of it."

Who were his favourite people as he was growing up?

"Gene McDaniels," he says, without hesitating. "He wrote a song called *One Hundred Pounds of Clay*. And it was the first song that I had heard that had the fourth chord in it. All the others just had the three -- C, F, and G. Then all of a sudden, this record came out that had A Minor, C, F, and G, and that really hit me strong. So that guy means a lot to me.

"And you know, I recently met him in New York. He was playing at a night club, and I went down to see him, and he recognized me from the Letterman show. So I said, 'Boy, that song, *One Hundred Pounds of Clay*, that really changed my life.' And he didn't believe me. He thought I was kidding because, you know, on TV I kid a lot, and say things that sound sincere, but which are totally insincere. So he didn't believe me.

"But I explained to him about that A Minor chord, and

7-4

114

7-5

then all of a sudden, he could tell that I knew what I was talking about. I was serious, and he got the picture."

Another influence was Del Shannon, who produced recordings with a very high background organ in them.

"There was a record called *The Runaway*," he says. "I think of it as classical music now. But there was an organ solo in that record that influenced me heavily.

"Recently, I played on a record by a group called Scandal. It was called *Good Bye to You*, and I was called upon to play an organ solo, and what I did was really an etude in Del Shannon. I played kind of my tribute to all of those records, with that same high organ sound that I was now able to get on a sophisticated synthesizer. You know, a $5,000 instrument to get a sound that Del Shannon probably got on a $500 chord organ."

By the time Paul Shaffer was growing up in the Lakehead, television was making headway.

"Of course, there was only one channel," he reminisces. "And Saturday night was Hockey Night in Canada, whether you liked it or not. But the Ed Sullivan Show was a very big event. Our whole family enjoyed it. And of course, I got a big kick out of the rock performers like the Four Seasons. I used to pay very close attention to them. They were white kids from New Jersey who were trying to emulate that wonderful black sound."

"They had the sound of a guy going up very high in a falsetto voice, and that was a black kind of innovation they used to do. That really reached me very deeply. I remember every appearance they ever made on the Sullivan show.

"I'm so tied to that era that since going to New York, I've made it my business to seek out some of these people that I grew up listening to, and quiz them a bit. What was it, or how did they do this or that? How did they make those records? And they get a little bit scared sometimes, because I know so much about them. I remember specific appearances they made on TV, which they can't even remember themselves."

While he was growing up here, and beginning to develop his talent, Paul sometimes worked with older local musicians. One in particular that he remembers and still respects is Roy Coran, whom he calls a real musi-

... I played kind of my tribute to all of those records ...

... the Ed Sullivan Show was a very big event ...

7-5 *The Bonnvilles, 1965*

115

... it'll be a wonderful opportunity for people to get to see real performers...

THE FOURTH DIMENSION

cal guy.

Paul is thrilled about the opening of our new Auditorium; thrilled that famous performers will finally come here so that Thunder Bay people can see them.

"When I was a kid," he recalls, "I saw Liberace in the Fort William Gardens. I saw the Beach Boys, too, and that was about it. They were really the only performers that ever came here. So now it'll be a wonderful opportunity for people to get to see real performers."

"I understand Mel Torme and Jack Jones will be coming, and that's fabulous. I never had that kind of opportunity here. So when I got to Toronto, I was a little shaky that first year. I made it through, but not really with flying colours, because I was so thrilled to be in a place where you could see real world class performers. I was going out every night to see these people. I was just so thrilled. It was all brand new to me because, up here, you just didn't get exposed to that at all."

However, when these people come to our new Auditorium, Mr. Shaffer hopes they get better treatment than he used to get.

"I just hope," he laughs, "that when Jack Jones finishes his set, the people applaud for him."

One of the many ports of call visited by folk music on its journey from swing and blues to acid rock, was the coffee houses. They flourished briefly in the early 60s, and provided an intimate venue wherein folk artists and their audiences could come together and communicate.

The one we had in Fort William was called the Fourth Dimension. It stood back behind the Royal Edward Hotel in a building that had been called the Club Seaway before Gordon Crompton and Don Merriman formed the partnership that made it work.

"It had been a place where you came with your bottle," says Gordon. "And when liquor licencing came, they couldn't get a licence, so they closed up. We took it over, and it was called a quiet house. There was no talking whatsoever while the show was on."

The 4D charged 25 cents per hour, plus whatever you ordered. They had a time clock which was punched when you came in, and again when you left.

"No drugs in those days," recalls Mr. Crompton. "No drinking problems. It was a clean house and a quiet house. The people pretty well conducted it themselves. There were a lot of people locally, who were interested in that folk music, and when the show started, there wasn't a sound in the place. You couldn't run a place like that today, because you'd have to police it too much."

CKPR's Ray Dee also remembers the Fourth Dimension, and the sort of entertainers it featured.

"All those coffee houses were exactly the same, interior-wise," he recalls. "Everything had to be black. The black originated I think with the Beatnik era, and seemed to symbolize escape, I suppose. But when you came to the door, you could never tell if there was anyone in there. They'd deliberately keep you waiting this side of the black curtain. I guess the idea was that there was always a certain amount of mystery."

The coffee house idea had come from the United States, as does most of our pop music, and it caught on quickly.

"There was still a certain amount of peace, and what-have-you from the 50s," says Ray. "There were no really big wars going on at the time, and the whole of North America seemed to be at some kind of level that's hard to define. I think this was one reason why these places sprang up. There was nothing for that group at the time.

"Artists like the Byrds were big in those days. Also Sonny Terry & Brownie McGee used to play the circuit. The Cryin' Shames was another group. I think one of their guys ended up with Crosby, Stills, Nash, and Young."

According to Gordon Crompton, there were two other Four-Ds. One was in Winnipeg, and the other in Regina.

"I knew the fellow who owned the one in Regina," says Gordon. "He happened to be a Kentucky Fried Chicken guy, so we had something in common. I also met the chap who had the one in Winnipeg. So we all hired each of the acts, and they'd play two weeks in each city. That way, we could get them quite reasonable."

"One of the more famous people that actually got started there," says Ray Dee, "was Neil Young. I managed him at the time, and

...Everything had to be black...

...One of the more famous people that actually got started there was Neil Young...

117

7-6 *Reebtones Dave Smythe and Randy Stewart rock the bandshell at Waverley Park, 1985*

7-7 *International star Bryan Adams meets his fans at Fort William Gardens, 1985*

7-8 *Tommy Horricks belts it out with Ronnie and the Comets, 1961*

recorded some of his early material with him. He came down here from Winnipeg with his band, and they were called Neil Young and the Squires."

Mr. Crompton points out that, in booking the entertainment, he had to provide room and board for the entertainers, and that didn't necessarily mean just the actual performers. It could include wives and children. At the time, he owned the Sea Breezes Motel on Cumberland, so he had a place to put them up.

"But opening night," he recalls, "the place was packed and the entertainment hadn't shown up. We were meeting every plane, and eventually, my friend Bill Antonyshyn got up and played his banjo, and we had a singalong, which turned out to be a common type of entertainment in the place -- singalongs."

The fad died very soon after it was born. Acts drew fewer and fewer people, and the club finally went broke. It was still there in 1965, but by then, its zenith had obviously passed.

7-7

7-8

8-1

# The Orchestra

GAS PUMPS? AH, NOWADAYS THEY'RE JUST BIG BOXES STUCK OUTside of service stations, lookin' like astronauts with their fingers in their ears. Why, folks don't even look at 'em while they're gettin' filled up, 'cause they're scared to. But at least they're built so's a car can smash into 'em without the whole place goin' up like a torch, and that's good, 'cause that very thing happened one afternoon over here at Long Lac.

Yes sir, back in the spring of '60, it was. March, I think. Seems these two musicians were hitchin' a free ride to Calgary by drivin' a car for this guy in Toronto. And just as they was pullin' into this here gas station at Long Lac, danged if they didn't hit some ice and slammed right into the gas pump. Made such a mess of the car that the last we seen of 'em, they was climbin' aboard the bus, headin' for the Lakehead.

Always wondered what happened to 'em . . .

James A. 'Bud' Martin, who has been involved with the Thunder Bay Symphony Orchestra almost since it organized, very well remembers what happened to them:

"These two young fellows -- Rene Charrier and Doug Dahlgren -- had to abandon their car at Long Lac, and come into Thunder Bay by bus. Well, they stayed at the Royal Edward Hotel, and the next day they asked somebody on the street how they could get to Port Arthur. The person replied that they'd have to take a bus, and they thought it was miles away. They didn't realize that the two were adjacent cities. One of the people they met was Saul Laskin, who was Mayor of Port Arthur at the time."

And Mr. Laskin recalls:

"It was a Saturday morning around ten o'clock, when these two stragglers came into the store. We were situated in the North Ward on Cumberland Street. At that time, I was handling very good pianos and organs, and I had an upright grand. There were quite a number of people in the store, shopping.

"These two young men came in, and as I say, they were a bit straggly, and looked a little thin. They didn't have many suitcases with them, and I'm sure they didn't have any money. They said, 'Can we practice?' and I said, 'Be my guest!'

"One sat at an organ and the other at the piano, and all of

*. . . **These two young fellows had to abandon their car at Long Lac** . . .*

8-1   Thunder Bay Symphony Orchestra and Chorus, 1975

... all of a sudden, there was a hush in the store ...

... They were convinced to stay ...

THE BIRTH

a sudden, there was a hush in the store. People stopped in their tracks. Music flowed like we'd never heard before. Beautiful music! I turned around. I couldn't believe what I had heard. And all of a sudden, all our customers started to mill around these two. It went on all afternoon. It was exciting, and people were coming in to listen!

"Well, we fed them and talked to them, and asked them what they were doing. They said they'd run into a little tough luck and had heard there was a need for piano teachers in this area. They felt they wanted to stay, but they really wanted to go west.

"I said, 'What do you want to go out west for?' And of course, I was selfish at that time. Being the Mayor of the city, I wanted these people here. They were convinced to stay after my firm assisted them financially, and we sold them a few pianos on spec, and subsidized them for a few months. Again I was selfish, because I wanted this community to have something that I felt we were lacking.

"Rene indicated to me that he had experience in conducting. Doug was an experienced pianist. Rene was also a very good organist, so he got a job playing in a church and so did Doug, to supplement their incomes, and they got some clients. They located on St. Paul Street, right over a pool room.

"Then Rene said he'd like to start an orchestra, and I looked at him and said, 'Come on!'. But he said he'd like to have a symphony orchestra, and that intrigued me, of course. So we got a few people together, and there was a call for musicians, and quite a number of people from the churches and the Boards of Education -- teachers -- started to gather around him."

"I remember one of their early practices in St. Andrews' Parish. I recall it very vividly. Oh, the first time they played *O Canada*, Oh man! ... Oh, man ..."

They called it the Lakehead Symphony Orchestra, and at its first concert in Lakeview High School Auditorium on Tuesday, November 29th, 1960, it boasted 40 players. The varied program concluded with Mr. Dahlgren performing the first movement of Tschaikowsky's Concerto No. 1 in B Flat Minor, Op. 23.

... Strings shrieked and squawked ...

... if it hadn't been for Rene and Doug, we'd still be searching ...

NO MONEY

Survivors say that the symphony got completely mixed up. Some of the musicians tried to transpose as they played what they thought Rene, who was conducting, wanted. Strings shrieked and squawked, woodwinds slithered and slobbered, the trombones fluttered into flatulence, and outside, one of the worst blizzards of all time hit the Lakehead. People could hardly get home afterwards, and some even had to check into hotels for the night.

BUT ... Something very special had happened there that evening, because what is now the very much superior Thunder Bay Symphony Orchestra had been born. A colicky baby to be sure, that obviously had only one direction to grow, but it has very steadily done that ever since, and with distinction.

The orchestra which Rene Charrier and Doug Dahlgren founded that year, wasn't the first in this community. As has already been said elsewhere in this publication, Gunton B. Smalley has that distinction, back in the 1920s. When he left in 1928, Mr. Albert Kennedy attempted to continue his work, but the group only performed two concerts and petered out. Arnold Phillips then drew together an orchestra which performed only once, and in 1939, Ralph Colossimo created the Thunder Bay Concert Orchestra which functioned for a few years. Following its demise in the 1940s, nothing more was done until the car hit that gas pump.

"I often look back and wonder whether Thunder Bay really was ready for a symphony," says Bud Martin. "But somebody had to seize the initiative, and I feel certain that if it hadn't been for Rene and Doug, we'd still be searching. But they got it going, and the next year, they decided they should have a Board of Directors. There were some very interesting people with us on that first Board, too. John Booth, a former Alderman, and Doug Fisher, Hubert Badanai, Ken McGray, and Gron Morgan, among several others."

Of course, nobody got paid. There were early attempts to bring that about, but with only ticket money to sustain it, pay cheques had to be held in abeyance until the orchestra could afford them.

"The Musicians' Union, rightly or wrongly, felt that the members of the orchestra should join them," recalls Saul Laskin, "and I see no

8-2

8-2 Dwight Bennett, Thunder Bay
Symphony Orchestra Conductor

. . . Players joked about expecting to see cows walk in . . .

HARRY BATEMAN

. . . We sold 600 season tickets not knowing whether there'd even be an orchestra . . .

fault in that. But there was an emergency call for me to come and talk to the group. I had an excellent conversation with the President of the Union at that time, and we both agreed that it was a little premature, that the important thing was to have an orchestra with some roots. And I credit the President and the Chairman of the Union at that time, that they recognized the situation and never bothered. And so the orchestra survived."

The orchestra received its legal letters patent in 1962 as the Lakehead Symphony Orchestra Association Incorporated, and became the Thunder Bay Symphony Orchestra Association Inc., with amalgamation in 1970. Thus it remains.

By the spring of 1964, the LSO was selling season tickets, and had moved from Lakeview High School to the Coliseum at the Canadian Lakehead Exhibition. Players joked about expecting to see cows walk in when anybody opened the door, but they couldn't help noticing that a lot of people opened the doors, came in, sat down and stayed. The orchestra had such solid support because Lakehead people wanted a symphony orchestra, and knew that the only way to accomplish this, was to come out and clap for the one they had. By today's standards, standing ovations came pretty easily in those days, and not a few prayers were said, especially when the orchestra aimed at a crescendo.

At the end of the 1963/64 season, Rene Charrier decided it was time to move on, so he left for Saskatchewan. Mr. Dahlgren remained for another 10 years.

"We already had a deficit by then," recalls Bud Martin. "It was $2,500 and that was big money in those days. So we didn't have a conductor, and we didn't know whether we'd have any musicians come out that fall, but we had faith in the orchestra. We went out and sold 600 season tickets for the next year, not knowing whether there'd even be an orchestra, because that was the kind of support we had."

Indeed, it was quite common during the orchestra's first decade, to mail out season tickets to Lakehead people without them having paid first. As many as 1,200 would go out in a season, with not more than a dozen or so remaining unpaid. The arrival of the tickets would remind people that it was time to send the orchestra some money, and they'd mail in their

8-3

8-4

cheques.

Providentially, at this point, along came Mr. C. H. 'Harry' Bateman, to teach instrumental music at Hammarskjold High School. The Symphony Board immediately prevailed upon him to conduct the LSO as well, and he served in both capacities until 1967. During his time, he founded the youth orchestra. Instruments and lessons were supplied to young students in the public and separate school systems. These students became the foundation of the youth orchestra -- which still functions -- and many of them have graduated to the senior orchestra.

"Harry had been a bandmaster with the Canadian Navy on the west coast," said the late J. Edison Gunn, the orchestra's first Concertmaster. "He was a very fine musician. Not a symphony man, but still a very fine musician who did the very best he could, and began some really good things. We all liked Mr. Bateman very much."

Someone else noted that Mr. Bateman did something else for this community, too, because until he came, Grand Marais used to win all the prizes at the Lakehead Musical Festival for bands. That stopped the year he came.

During Harry Bateman's tenure, the LSO sponsored a concert by the Toronto Symphony under Seija Ozawa, at the Fort William Gardens. It was highly successful. The orchestra brought in its first guest artist in 1966, Lorand Fenyves. This paved the way for visits from other eminent artists such as Maureen Forrester, Lois Marshall, Anton Kuerti, and Lili Kraus.

In 1967, Mr. Bateman relinquished the podium to Boris Brott, and continued as Assistant Conductor until 1968. Mr. Brott, a distinguished member of an outstanding Canadian musical family, also headed the Music Department at Lakehead University, and organized the first Symphony School of Music. While he was Conductor of the LSO, Mr. Brott also headed an orchestra in England, and then the Hamilton Symphony, and served a season as Associate Conductor of the New York Philharmonic, with Leonard Bernstein.

In 1969, the musicians-in-residence program was started, whereby the orchestra engaged the Princeton String Quartet to perform and to teach full time for the association. Indeed, the Princeton Quartet were the

... he founded the youth orchestra ...

WHAT BORIS BROUGHT

8-3 Dennis Brott appears with the Lakehead Symphony Orchestra as guest cellist

8-4 J. Crittall, B. Brott, H. Knights, W. Harris

...*My God! This Symphony is operating in the black!*...

```
┌─CALENDAR OF COMING EVENTS─┐
│                           │
│ Feb. 18    2:00 p.m.  THUNDER BAY SYMPHONY ORCHESTRA
│                       Schroeder's Favourites Children's Concert
│                       Selkirk Auditorium
│ Feb. 15-   8:00 p.m.  Cambrian Players -- "My Three Angels"
│      18               University Centre Theatre
│ Feb. 18    3:30 p.m.  ORMTA (Fort William Branch) Piano recital
│                       Mary J. Black Library
│ Feb. 22-   9:00 a.m.  Lakehead Music Festival
│ Mar. 3    10:00 p.m.  Faculty of Education and Selkirk
│ Feb. 23    8:00 p.m.  THUNDER BAY CHAMBER PLAYERS
│                       University Centre Theatre
│ Feb. 23-   6:30 p.m.  Fort William Male Choir
│      24-              Singalong Smorgasbord
│      25               DaVinci Centre
│ Feb. 26   10:30 a.m.  T.B.S.O. MARATHON -- C.K.P.R.
│ Feb. 26    2:00 p.m.  Finnish Folk Dancers
│                       Kalevala Day Celebrations
│                       Finlandia Club
│ Feb. 26    8:15 p.m.  THUNDER BAY YOUTH SYMPHONY ORCHESTRA
│                       Fac. of Education
│ Mar. 2-    8:00 p.m.  Magnus Theatre -- "The Caretaker"
│      11
│ Mar. 5     8:30 p.m.  THUNDER BAY SYMPHONY ORCHESTRA
│                       Candlelight Concert
│                       Royal Edward Hotel
│ Mar. 7-               National Exhibition Centre
│      26               Nature Photography by four local photographers
│ Mar. 11-   8:00 p.m.  Finnish Folk Dancers -- Concert
│      12               Finlandia Club
│ Mar. 11-   2:00 p.m.  THUNDER BAY SYMPHONY ORCHESTRA
│      12               CELEBRITY CONCERT -- Soloist MAUREEN FORRESTER
│            3:00 p.m.  Selkirk Auditorium
│ Mar. 12    8:00 p.m.  Prosvita Ladies Choir
│                       Shevchenko Anniversary Concert
│                       Prosvita Hall
│ Mar. 16    8:15 p.m.  ORMTA (Fort William Branch) Piano Recital
│                       Mary J. Black Library
│ Mar. 17    8:00 p.m.  Cambrian Players "Wacousta"
│                       -- by Ne'er-do-Well Players
│                       Selkirk Auditorium
│ Mar. 19    8:00 p.m.  THUNDER BAY CHAMBER PLAYERS
│                       University Centre Theatre
│ Mar. 20-              Fire, Earth and Fibre -- Juried show
│ Apr. 21               Confederation College
│ Mar. 25    8:00 p.m.  THUNDER BAY SYMPHONY ORCHESTRA
│      26               AND CHORUS
│                       Bach's St. John Passion
│                       St. Paul's United Church
│ Mar. 30               National Exhibition Centre
│                       Human Landscape -- Local Artists
│ Mar. 30-   8:00 p.m.  Magnus Theatre "Equus"
│ Apr. 8
│ Apr. 7     8:00 p.m.  THUNDER BAY SYMPHONY ORCHESTRA
│      8                DuMaurier Promenade Concert -- Liona Boyd
│                       St. Patrick's Auditorium
└───────────────────────────┘
   8-5
```

128

only professional musicians in the orchestra at that time.

"I remember when Boris came," says Bud Martin, "because the first thing he did was look at our financial statements. And he said, 'My God! This Symphony is operating in the black! A successful symphony never operates in the black. You always operate at a deficit!' So, under Boris's guidance, we became a very successful symphony orchestra, because we quickly had a deficit.

"But you know, as I say, maybe we shouldn't have had a symphony here at that time, because we didn't have the musicians. So we had to get professional help from Duluth, and sometimes from Hamilton. But you have to give Boris credit for the energy he had. I think he established the quality that this audience expects today. He brought in artists like Lili Kraus and Maureen Forrester, and where else would a community of this size be able to hear talent like that?

"I remember bringing a Grade Five or Six class from McKenzie to see Lili, because they wanted to meet an artist, and I couldn't have picked a better person. She had spent many years in a Japanese prisoner-of-war camp, and she didn't know, then, whether she'd ever be able to play the piano again, because of what they made her do. And she spoke to these kids in such an open way that it was just a beautiful experience for them.

"I think Lili came here twice with Boris. And one of the times, he had given a lecture at the University Theatre in which he told an interesting little story . . . something about Sir Thomas Beecham having rehearsed an orchestra for one piano concerto, and the guest artist rehearsing another. They didn't discover this until they came together on stage. And Boris ended by saying, 'But those things never happen now'.

"Well, a day or two later, he had a rehearsal of the orchestra and Lili came in later that evening and met with Boris. It must have been a Thursday night. They had coffee at the hotel, and during the conversation, they mentioned the concerto. And Boris said, 'But Lili, you're not playing *that* concerto. It's *this* one that you're playing!'

"So I remember Lili Kraus saying, 'Well, okay. I haven't played that one for some time. Maybe I can still do it properly. If I can't, we'll

OUR MEXICAN GENTLEMAN

DWIGHT BENNETT

... one of Canada's most brilliant young conductors ...

8-5 Thunder Bay Symphony Newsletter "Calendar of Events", February-March, 1978

just have to do a different one.' So I also remember Boris coming up here to my house on a Friday night, sitting right there at my table, and phoning C.B.C. Toronto, Winnipeg, New York -- all over the world -- to get the music for the other concerto that she had prepared for the concert.

"And this orchestra! This group of amateurs plus a string quartet! He called an early rehearsal on the Saturday morning, and they rehearsed it. Then they did it in the afternoon with Lili Kraus, and they put on the concert that night and Sunday at Selkirk, and nobody knew what had happened!

"But, you see, that was the sort of thing that Boris could do. And you know, who else could do it but Boris Brott?"

Manuel Suarez became the orchestra's fourth Conductor in 1972, when Mr. Brott moved to Hamilton.

"Manuel, I think, was Concertmaster of the National Orchestra of Mexico," said Edison Gunn. "He was hired as Conductor, of course, and Manuel just . . . he put in the glue. He wasn't a symphonic conductor as such. He's a marvellous violinist, and he had a warmth, a rapport, with the members of the orchestra. Just solid. I mean, we loved him, and he conducted well. But he kept that orchestra together, and gave it something very worthwhile."

In 1974, Mr. Dwight Bennett stepped to our podium. Hailed as one of Canada's most brilliant young conductors, Mr. Bennett began his musical studies at an early age, earning three degrees from the University of Toronto. He has worked with some of the world's most eminent maestros, including Karel Ancerl, Victor Feldbrill, Elmer Iseler, Ernesto Barbini, and Franz Paul Decker in Toronto; Tibor Kozma in Bloomington, Indiana; Kiril Kondrashin in Holland; Franco Ferrara in Italy; and Bernard Baitink in Great Britain.

In his first conducting post, Mr. Bennett was conductor of the University of Toronto Repertoire Orchestra and the North York Chorus. Doctoral studies took him to Indiana University where he was an associate instructor and conductor of the Pro Arte Ensemble, the Symphony Orchestra, and the Opera Theatre.

As with Boris Brott, Dwight was also named Director of

Music at Lakehead University.

Here are his reminiscences on what he found in Thunder Bay:

"When I arrived here, the orchestra was in a state of stasis. They had begun with Mr. Dahlgren and company on a community basis only, and purely amateur. Then, during the years of Boris Brott, they had decided to experiment with the musicians in residence concept, and had brought in a few people. They had also augmented the amateur orchestra with professionals from out of town.

"The point, I guess, in looking at it from this vantage point, was to interest the community in having a more professional orchestra by just trying it for a couple of years on an import basis. That interest took hold to a degree, but it was coupled with a financial problem, because the cost of that importing was severe; it was in the order of a $40,000 deficit at that time.

"So Boris went on to other things, and they had Manuel come. Manuel was caught in the position of big deficit and the Board wanting to hold things. They believed in the dream, but they didn't see how they could do it yet. The audience dropped off, the orchestra reverted back to almost exclusively amateur, with four professionals, but without a real clear plan as to what it was trying to do.

"Then I came here and we started both things. We tried to develop a professional corps of musicians, and we built a management team to run the symphony with the Board. We had a huge success in the first two years, growing from about 250 subscribers to 1,200. Just an unbelievable growth.

"That was due to the fact that the community was ready to have something good. They wanted to have their own orchestra that could play well. It wasn't playing well, and they knew it. And they didn't want to support that sort of thing.

"Our first concerts went very well. Certainly not like it is now, but it was, by comparison, quite good. And it seemed to have a direction. That's the word I was getting back; that whatever was out of place didn't matter, because the orchestra seemed to be a going concern.

8-6 *Chorus rehearses "Missa Solemnis" by Beethoven, accompanied by Heather Morrison, 1980*

8-7 *Chorus intonates Bach's "Christmas Oratorio" at St. Andrew's Roman Catholic Church, 1981*

8-8 *Thunder Bay Symphony Orchestra and Chorus perform in Beaver Brae Auditorium, Kenora, 1983*

. . . They believed in the dream . . .

8-6

8-7

8-8

THE ORCHESTRA TODAY

8-9 *"Music to pay bills by"* —
*Symphony members on location at
City Hall*

8-10 *In concert at Selkirk
Auditorium, 1985*

"Then we attracted a number of young professionals to come here, to share this dream that we could have a small chamber orchestra, professional corps, in a larger community orchestra. Then the subscriptions took a big jump, and the Board committed a lot of money to develop a professional corps and staff, and begin developing."

Upon arriving in Thunder Bay, Mr. Bennett, noting the large number of excellent choirs already here, immediately organized the Symphony Chorus. Now numbering some 120 mixed voices, this volunteer chorus gives four performances per year, featuring works in the orchestra's choral repertoire. The chorus frequently accompanies the corps musicians on orchestral tours in the region, and is as well received as the TBSO at all of them.

Other ventures instigated by Dwight include the Thunder Bay Music Camp, which provides an immersion-type musical environment for well over 100 regional students every summer. He also began the Music School, in which the professional musicians taught individual pupils. This succeeded so well that it had to be disbanded in recent years, because it became much more efficient for the musicians to teach privately in their own way.

And by getting out into the region, the TBSO has begun to evolve into a truly regional orchestra. It now has area citizens serving as Board members, there is fund raising for the orchestra throughout the region, and the permanent musicians frequently give special recitals, hold workshops, and otherwise augment the music programs now growing in the smaller communities.

"We now do as many as three tours a year," says Dwight, "proving again and again that there's an interest and a need out there in the region. We go all the way to Kapuskasing and Wawa, and west to the Manitoba boundary, and there's a tremendous response all the way.

"Another area that has just opened recently is Manitoba. There are six communities up there that want us. The whole province isn't being serviced because the Winnipeg Symphony is just too busy. We're exploring that, and it's costly, but the Canada Council's interested, because we'll be going inter-provincial. We're also being approached to visit Saskatchewan, since it isn't that much farther if we're already visiting, say, western Manitoba.

8-10

A TIME OF GROWTH

"So there's interest outside our region, and in our two funding bodies -- Provincial and Federal -- that we tour, extensively. The only caveat is that it doesn't cost, that it's an asset to this community."

As Thunder Bay's audience has noticed of late, the variety of the orchestra's repertoire has considerably broadened. We now have five other series besides the main concerts, through which to touch as many tastes as possible.

"We're planning much farther ahead, too," adds Dwight, "and will plan two years ahead henceforth. That will allow us to properly prepare our tours and commit us to a variety of programming that we know will work. The key to it is diversity. There are audiences out there, and on one night, a person might want something serious, whereas at another time, the same person will want something much lighter."

Mr. Bennett also sees more work with local groups and local artists. He's already looking toward operas again, and the possibility of musical theatre with Magnus.

"The idea is to put the two professional groups in town together," he says. "We've done things with the amateur groups -- the musicians, certainly have -- but we haven't done much with Magnus."

The advent of the new Auditorium, he points out, will greatly help the orchestra's musicians, because they will be needed many times at the facility. Also, because of the presence of a professional orchestra, some shows can call on Thunder Bay which otherwise could not, despite the new Auditorium.

"The way it works," he says, "is to rehearse in the morning and perform at night. Our people can do that, but a city like Regina, which has only a community orchestra, can't. They can't rehearse during the day at all, and we can."

Looking back on what he has seen during his time in Thunder Bay, Mr. Bennett speaks enthusiastically:

"It's incredible. There has been such growth in myself, in the orchestra, and in the community. It began with great enthusiasm when I came here. Just an incredible willingness and energy to try to do something. We weren't always clear what we were trying to do, but there was such a great pride here, and there still is.

"People here really support where they live, like nowhere else that I've known. It's part of the isolation and the climate. Some people say there isn't anything here, you know, but that's really not accurate. To compare Thunder Bay with many other cities that are our size or slightly smaller, things are pretty good here.

"So I would say the most important thing that has happened is the growth in our product. The orchestra itself has grown to be very good in quality. And that attracts supporters and volunteers and an audience. People want to support something that's good.

"We have a good team and a good orchestra. It's one of the most important assets of the community, just like the Auditorium. The morale is excellent, and there's enthusiasm, and we have vitality here. The community is much more active musically.

"Thunder Bay will not let this orchestra go, and neither will the governments. There's a high priority out there. There are many orchestras in southern Ontario, but we're getting good increases in grants when others aren't getting any.

"We're looking at making recordings and we're on the edge of getting some C.B.C. broadcasts, and all of that is regional development, too.

"But what we want to do here is build the best of its kind or genre in Canada, and I think it's possible. For every negative you can put on our community because of its size, there is also a positive, and because of where we are, we don't have any competition. We can therefore develop in our own way. We can be unique.

"Thunder Bay is really a lovely place to live. You won't find audiences more dedicated than they are right here. You can get them bigger -- and that's our problem, as an orchestra -- but no more supportive. And so we have to go out and knock on doors, and then when people come to hear us, they must be able to say, 'Hey! That was good! We didn't hear all those missed notes like we used to'.

"And in this new Auditorium of ours, they will hear this excellent orchestra as it should really be heard."

... there was such a great pride here, and there still is ...

... what we want to do here is build the best of its kind ...

8-11 *Thunder Bay Symphony Orchestra perform their "Best of Broadway", Selkirk Auditorium, 1985*

8-11

9-1

9-2

9-3

9-4

The Auditorium

The Auditorium

... the performing arts themselves remained aloof from one another ...

9-1 Stage lift area, January 1984

9-2 Foundation complete, January 1984

9-3 Proscenium arch is the first steel, January 1984

9-4 Second stage with side steel for boxes, January 1984

AT LAST, OUR NEW AUDITORIUM IS A REALITY.

So many people, great and humble, citizens of Thunder Bay, Northwestern Ontario, and from all over Canada, collectively deserve a prolonged standing ovation for their patience, determination, and very hard work. Without all of them -- and right here, in this city, there were thousands -- we might still be waiting.

And we have waited 14 long years.

Our Auditorium has taken such a very long time to be built, of course, because of politics, public opinion, and several economic oscillations, but also because for many years, nobody had a clear conception of what we needed, or wanted, or could afford. For ever so long, we didn't think we needed such a place at all.

But there was something else, too. For a needlessly long time, the performing arts themselves, having long since matured to excellence in both cities, remained aloof from one another. Very often, the one would have nothing to do with the other, even within the same discipline. Even now, jealousies still surface, and particular groups keep very much to themselves, when a detached observer might wish that all of them could simply feel proud to be part of the cultural milieu that is uniquely Thunder Bay, and work for its betterment.

Now at least, there is the means of generating dialogue and joint action, without which having got started, there might not have been an auditorium at all. Surely the impetus had to come from the performers, themselves. It really couldn't begin down in the audience.

The talk of an auditorium didn't begin until well into this century. Even after World War II, music teachers easily presented their pupils in recital in churches. Major musical events and even musical festivals were held in churches. The lower halls accommodated plays and even dance recitals, and for variety shows, there were the old vaudeville theatres like the *Orpheum*, or the *Lyceum*, or the high schools. And for pageants, well, you used the Fort William Gardens, or the Port Arthur Arena; sometimes even the parks and the streets, and as long as things went along like that, who needed an auditorium?

Meanwhile, schools were enlarged, old halls renovated or

... Few paid attention to things like acoustics ...

EARLY EXCELLENCE

... Serious music was being taught and performed in both cities ...

torn down and new ones built, and like many other North American cities, Fort William and Port Arthur acquired a diverse collection of great big rooms, some nicer than others. Few paid attention to things like acoustics, creature comforts or accessibility, and certainly not parking. The paramount considerations seem to have been economy and adaptability. In those days, the emphasis was upon facilities that could serve a multitude of functions and be built cheaply. Thus, we inherited our legacy of bits and pieces -- as did most other cities -- each with its own unique assortment of virtues and vices. None was ideally suited even for the commonest performances of their day, never mind the complexities of the 1980s.

Yet even as far back as the 1920s, men like Gunton Smalley and Wilfred Coulson, and women like Mary Campbell and Mabel Airth were achieving excellence right here. There was a Philharmonic Society and two or three superb choirs. Serious music was being taught and performed in both cities, and being presented with finesse. We even had a choir or two, in those days, that sang in cities far removed from here, and were acclaimed by their audiences. And so it was about that time that suggestions began to be made about building a proper auditorium.

Of course, very few really understood the meaning of 'proper auditorium', and so the suggestions remained just that. Besides, where might such a place be built? Which city would get it? And how would it ever pay for itself if it sat idle most of the time? Very few shows toured the country by then. Motion pictures and radio were coming on very strong, and in the Depression, who would pay the price of admission when Jack Benny, Charlie McCarthy or Fibber McGee could be had for nothing?

The performing arts groups hadn't begun talking to one another yet, and so if anyone had asked local artists what kind of a facility should be built, he would have heard some very conflicting ideas, because the ideal venue for a meso soprano differs considerably from that for a prima ballerina. And whereas a symphony orchestra or opera might prefer a large hall, a theatre company performs best in a smaller, more intimate setting. On the other hand, a solo instrumentalist in recital, or a string quartet, or even a magician may prefer the comfort of a well ordered salon, while a pipe organist really needs a cathedral, and a pipe band is heard to best advantage only in the great outdoors.

We had almost all of those in 1929. Today, we have more than that, and occasionally get things like rock concerts, too, which couldn't even be imagined when the last hall was built here.

After the war, many developments occurred, several of which could be called milestones on the way to the auditorium. At the beginning of 1945, a Port Arthur committee headed by Alderman T.J. McAuliffe began pushing the idea. By the end of the year, an architect's sketch of a proposed facility had been prepared. It was to be a multi-use building. The auditorium would occupy the top floor, with a swimming pool in the lower. Total estimated cost was $2 million, and despite a publicity campaign by the Port Arthur Jaycees (Junior Chamber of Commerce, in those days), citizens voted it down in the municipal elections of January, 1946.

Within the next few years, two amateur theatre companies were formed -- the Fort William Little Theatre and the Community Players of Port Arthur, and so the two cities began to enjoy regular and excellent live theatre. In 1956, construction began on Lakehead University, which created a new 350-seat theatre for community use. The Lakehead Symphony Orchestra was organized in 1960, and there was formed in 1964, a committee of concerned citizens which called itself the Lakehead School of Fine Arts.

During the early 60s, a number of citizens had begun to notice that there was a growing shortage of instrumental instructors in both cities. Plenty of learning opportunities existed for piano, violin and voice, but very little for anything else. Accordingly, people from the Lakehead Symphony Orchestra, the Parks and Recreation Department of the City of Port Arthur, the Registered Music Teachers' Association, the Cambrian Players, the Lakehead Choral Group, a couple of dance schools and the Lakehead Music Festival formed the Lakehead School of Fine Arts, and ran it very successfully for three summers.

Its first sessions were held in the summer of 1965, and it disbanded at the end of the 1967 sessions. The venture used the University's facilities and was financed very largely by the Community Programs Branch of the Ontario Department of Education. Therefore, the LSFA was able to charge students very little, and bring in top notch instructors. Student ages

MAJOR MILESTONES

... At the beginning of 1945, a Port Arthur committee began pushing the idea ...

ranged right across three generations, and they took courses in painting, sculpture, instrumental music, ballet and theatre.

Dusty Miller was its first President, and its Board of Directors included Jean Crittall, Bud Martin, Ray Wittenburg, Ollie Sawchuck, Mrs. Orville Knight, Don McKinnon, Mrs. Mildred Gunn and Harry Myhal.

Mr. Martin recalls that Betty Oliphant of the National Ballet School was one of the instructors. Adrian Pecknold, acclaimed as an outstanding mime artist in theatre, did a course in his field. Natalie Kuzmich taught cello; Malcolm Tait, Principal Cellist with the Toronto Symphony, and Tayochi Tsumi, Resident musician at the University of Western Ontario, also taught cello. Several other noted artists in their fields, were attracted here during those summer sessions, to teach students from all over the region, and beyond.

In 1967, the Lakehead School of Fine Arts disbanded for several reasons, but mainly because Confederation College had come on stream by then, and the University was expanding. There was, says one, a great deal of volunteer burnout, and it was hoped -- and suggested -- that either or both of the senior institutions would pick up what the volunteers felt they could no longer provide. And so the program expired.

However, although they disbanded the summer school, the same groups, as a Centennial Project, cooperatively presented *Brigadoon* in 1967. From that came the Lakehead Amateur Music Productions which, in the years immediately following, staged: *Oklahoma, Kismet, My Fair Lady* and *Guys and Dolls*. Lakehead audiences loved them all.

"But there was a legacy from all this," says Dusty Miller. "Before the LSFA got going, each performing group was very separate. There was almost no cross over or communication, say, between a dance group or a music group or a theatre group. And the fact that we all got together and got to know each other, was an enormous help, because we came to recognize that we had many similar problems."

Thus, from all those people who worked together on the five musicals, there evolved a committee of seven, to formulate detailed proposals for a comprehensive arts organization. They were: Jean Crittall, Jim Foulds, Dusty Miller, Sister Marie, Rob McCormick, Ray Wittenburg, and

9-5 *Roof on completed steel framework. Note the observer on the lower right side of the skeleton, Spring 1984*

9-6 *Front entrance covered with sloped roof, July 1984*

9-7 *Studs and insulation 'layered' onto exterior, July 1984*

9-8 *Masonry work on west side of building, August 1984*

. . . There was a great deal of volunteer burnout . . .

THE GROUP OF SEVEN

9-7

9-8

Betty Goodings. They met very frequently throughout the winter and brought their ideas to a meeting of visual and performing arts groups in May, 1969, which brought about the formation of the Lakehead Council of the Arts. Mrs. Dusty Miller was its first Chairman.

The LCA included more than just arts people. There were representatives from business, labour, and both Boards of Education. It became an organization of anybody interested in the arts, not just those who actually practised them. And one of the major concerns that quickly emerged was the need for some kind of a performance and viewing centre.

It should be pointed out, however, that the LCA wasn't a group that merely wanted to lobby for an arts centre. Its member organizations pooled talents and presented arts circuses, summer schools, and even sponsored operas. But it will most likely be remembered longest for its auditorium crusade.

The LCA also discussed such mutual problems as loaning equipment, costumes, and expertise among member groups. It looked into the unique faults of the various performance venues, and served as a clearing house through which member groups could avoid scheduling events on the same evening, as was frequently happening. And it was from the LCA that emerged the 'wish list' regarding the kind of performance and viewing facility that would be of most benefit to the new city of Thunder Bay.

Because the LCA included painters and sculptors as well as musicians, dancers and actors, the envisioned facility was called a 'complex'. It would include a large auditorium, a small theatre, various rehearsal rooms, and a display space for the visual arts people. And because discussions about the 'complex' quickly began to occupy the major portion of LCA meetings, they formed a special Auditorium Committee. Dan O'Gorman was its first Chairman.

But even before this happened, funds began to trickle in. At one of the meetings, someone pointed out how impossible it would be to convince politicians of the need for an auditorium, unless the performing arts themselves did something positive by way of commitment. And so, groups such as the Fort William Male Choir, the Cambrian Players, the Lakehead Choral Group, and several others gave the proceeds of one of their shows to

the Sound of Men!
Otava (Finnish) Male Choir
The Lakehead Ukrainian Male Choir
The Fort William Male Choir
OCTOBER 17, 1970
— COLISEUM —
"Help The Auditorium Fund Grow"

9-9

the Lakehead Council of the Arts, to be used as 'seed money' to start the auditorium. Thus, when Mr. O'Gorman accepted the chairmanship, his committee already had a bank account.

Telling the full story of all that befell the Auditorium in the 14 long years it took to get built, could easily fill a volume in itself. For that information, please consult the pamphlet entitled *A History*, prepared by Mr. Clint Kuschak of the Auditorium staff, and available through his office. Nevertheless, some of the highlights can be touched upon.

The Thunder Bay Arts Complex was incorporated on September 3rd, 1971, as a charitable organization. Its name was changed on May 6th, 1983, to the Thunder Bay Community Auditorium Inc. The change aptly indicates what happened to the original idea on its long journey from dream to reality, for what began as an ideal arts facility, conceived by experienced artists and performers, was gradually scaled down to a more affordable performance auditorium only.

During the years 1972 and 1973, the initial feasibility studies were done, which confirmed that a new facility was required, that support for such a venture existed in the community, and that the necessary financing could be found. City Council approved the funding formula by which the three levels of government would each contribute about a third of the capital outlay -- the City's portion to include all funds acquired through public donations. The cost of the project, originally estimated to be $12 million, was revised to $15 million in November, 1974. As of the end of June, 1985 -- eleven years later -- the final bill was expected to be $14.5 million.

The first actual commitment of capital, however, didn't materialize until 1976. It came from the Province of Ontario, following the advent of Wintario.

"And even though we went through four Ministers of Citizenship and Culture," says Project Manager Clint Kuschak, "the commitment remained solid. They never went back on it all through the problems we had. They could easily have dropped it through the plebiscite, or even through the OMB hearing. But they didn't, and we're all very grateful that they stuck by us."

The City of Thunder Bay had committed itself, too, but

THE CAMPAIGN BEGINS

... what began as an ideal arts facility was gradually scaled down ...

9 9   *Helping the Auditorium Fund grow, 1970*

143

...the project more or less marked time...

...The TBAC Inc. finally received the $3 million...

SEATS, DOORS, RUGS AND FOUNTAINS

9-10 *Stage and lift opening areas, September 1984*

only on condition that the other two governments did likewise, and so, because the Federal Government refused any commitment until March 30th, 1981, nothing financially concrete could happen. The Committee couldn't even begin its fund raising drive, so the project more or less marked time for 10 years, waiting for the go-ahead from Ottawa, getting moved a total of three times, and responding to a plethora of studies, surveys, concerns and trivia.

On January 28th, 1980, the Hon. David MacDonald, Secretary of State in the Clark Government, announced that Ottawa would allocate $3 million for the auditorium's construction. Accordingly, on March 24th, the committee launched its Building Fund Campaign at a dinner in the Da Vinci Centre. By then, the government had fallen and an election campaign was in progress. Three weeks later, when balloting returned the Liberals to power, the new Secretary of State, the Hon. Francis Fox, was asked about the Auditorium grant. He couldn't give a firm decision date, and so the Building Fund campaign had to be suddenly suspended.

In November, the same Mr. Fox introduced a new program of cultural initiatives, which included capital financing for building projects. The TBAC Inc. immediately reapplied for its grant, and on Monday, March 30th, 1981, finally received the $3 million commitment from Ottawa. The Building Fund Campaign resumed immediately, and by year end had acquired pledges of $800,000.

The Building Fund was a two-pronged effort, one being called Key Donors, and the other Seat Endowments. The former sought donations, principally from businesses and foundations, for the various functional pieces that go into an auditorium. Such things as doors, washrooms, elevators, the public address system, lighting, and so on. All of them were donated, thanks to a great many local, regional, and national business firms. A good number of Trusts and Foundations also contributed, as did local clubs, lodges and other organizations. It was at this point, for instance, that the I.O.D.E. -- the first group ever to specifically allocate money towards the Auditorium -- donated its accumulated trust fund, and bought the piano.

The other division, called Seat Endowment, appealed to individuals and groups, and sold all of the available seats at $500 apiece. During this same time, the seat patron program was being successful in endowing the loge seats for $2,500 each. This campaign, too, was fully subscribed. Many families purchased more than one seat. Organizations bought blocks of them. The Fort William Male Choir, through individual member purchases, took an entire row, right across the auditorium.

Beginning in the fall of 1983, a 'Buy a Block' campaign also got under way, and people were asked to purchase blocks for $25 each. Again, various groups, associations, clubs, societies and individuals bought them. But donations had been coming in ever since the committee organized, and so it has transpired that many sources in Thunder Bay have given to this auditorium, and not just a few have given several times over. Such was the support behind this project. And when you add to all that, the millions of hours of work done by thousands of volunteers, the amount given becomes vastly greater.

Once the Building Fund got underway, proceeds went directly into construction or furnishing. But in the initial years, donations paid for the vital organization and planning that had to be done before the long process could even get started, and somehow had to be paid for.

"We kept receiving donations," recalls Dan O'Gorman, "and the donors felt that these should go into bricks and mortar. But we needed money right then to do the ground work on the idea, itself. Because, if we didn't do those things right, we'd never even get to the bricks and mortar."

By the middle of 1982, the Building Fund totalled $1.3 million. At this time, the official confirmations of the Federal and Provincial commitments were received, with an initial payment. On April 21st, the Hon. Bruce McCaffrey, Minister of Citizenship and Culture, announced Ontario's share to be $4.7 million, from Wintario, Access, and C.R.C.A. grant programs. By year's end, the Building Fund had reached $1,454,000 and the City's application to fund and construct the venture, had been approved by the Ontario Municipal Board.

As 1983 began, the project's Management Committee pressed Council for permission to proceed. The working drawings were ready, the capital estimates complete, and a reasonable financing plan developed. The TBCA Inc. proposed that a Construction Management Committee be formed, comprised of City Councillors, City Administrators, and TBCA Inc.

9-10

THE FINALE

9-11

9-12

members. This committee would undertake the management of the project through construction in the public interest.

This proposal led to the holding of a special Council meeting at which TBCA officials defended, once again, every conceivable aspect of the project that had been repeatedly justified every step of the way. During this period, too, the project was subjected to an Environmental Assessment Hearing, and passed this test successfully. But when the TBCA Inc., asked for permission to call tenders, Council decided to grant approval or not grant it, based on the results of a plebiscite to be held on Monday, June 20th, 1983. The question on the ballot read: *Are you in favour of the construction of a Community Auditorium in the city of Thunder Bay?* It required only a simple majority to pass.

Meanwhile, eight tenders were received by the 3:00 p.m. deadline of Friday, June 10th. They were publicly opened at the Canada Games Complex, and came in reasonably close to the anticipated $15 million figure.

At the announcement of the plebiscite, Auditorium volunteers felt depressed. They had been through several solicitations on behalf of the project already, and now here was another campaign for support that would have to be mounted.

Debby Krupa, a member of the Auditorium staff at the time, recalls their reactions:

"Some saw it as good news that once and for all, it would be settled. If we won, there would be no more controversy over it. Others were worried that we didn't have enough time to organize for the vote. A great many were at the point of burn out, and it was going to take extra strength to pull it all together.

"But what it boiled down to was either the community wanted an auditorium, or it didn't. We felt sure the people did want it, or we wouldn't have done so well financially."

On the night of the vote, the committee rented one of the Oak Rooms at the Red Oak Inn, to monitor the results, and an air of excitement prevailed as the polls began reporting. Right from the start, everyone could see it would be close, but they felt confident. And then it began to lose.

9-11 *Exterior skin encloses the building, October 1984*

9-12 *Main floor of audience chamber is poured, December 1984*

9-13 *Orchestra pit lift system, March 1985*

... Are you in favour of the construction of a Community Auditorium in the City of Thunder Bay? ...

9-13

Volunteers, feeling depresed, started calling the event a 'slash-our-wrists party'. However, as the evening wore on and the final count drew nearer, they could see that the vote was pulling slightly in favour, and the mood quickly changed to one of elation and optimism.

"When it just squeaked by," says Debby, "everybody did a bit of soul searching. Maybe if we had been organized better, we would have got more votes. And yet, was that really what we had been looking for? Shouldn't it have been that the people, themselves, had to make their own decisions, rather than merely being urged to vote?

"We could have done more to push them to the polls, maybe, but we couldn't have done more to bring the Auditorium to the public. And really, if they didn't want it, then they had their right to say so.

"I think that's pretty much how the evening ended. Yes, the Auditorium had been approved by a very thin majority, and once it came, there would still be a lot of pain, but perhaps we had the opportunity through audience development to make sure it was successful."

The plebiscite had given approval by only 327 votes, but it had passed, and so, on August 31st, Ball Brothers of Kitchener -- the same people who had built Kitchener's very similar Centre-In-The-Square -- was awarded the contract. Sod was turned in late September by quite a number of local citizens, each supplying his or her own shovel, and by the end of October, 50% of the foundation was complete. Steel began to rise in December, by which time the Building Fund stood at $1.939 million.

As 1984 began, the new Auditorium was taking shape in the skyline of Thunder Bay. At first, it was merely a yellow steel skeleton, standing 27 metres high. But throughout 1984 and 1985, it gradually assumed its final profile as various layers of skin were added: the profile that it will carry well into the next century.

"The project is very close to the Kitchener one in design," says General Manager Brian McCurdy, "and I think Kitchener's is one of the best facilities in Canada. Ours had the same consultants and builders. The core building is very similar, except that ours is about 300 seats smaller.

"When I first arrived, it was pretty much just a skeleton although still impressive at that point. My first impression, even at that primi-

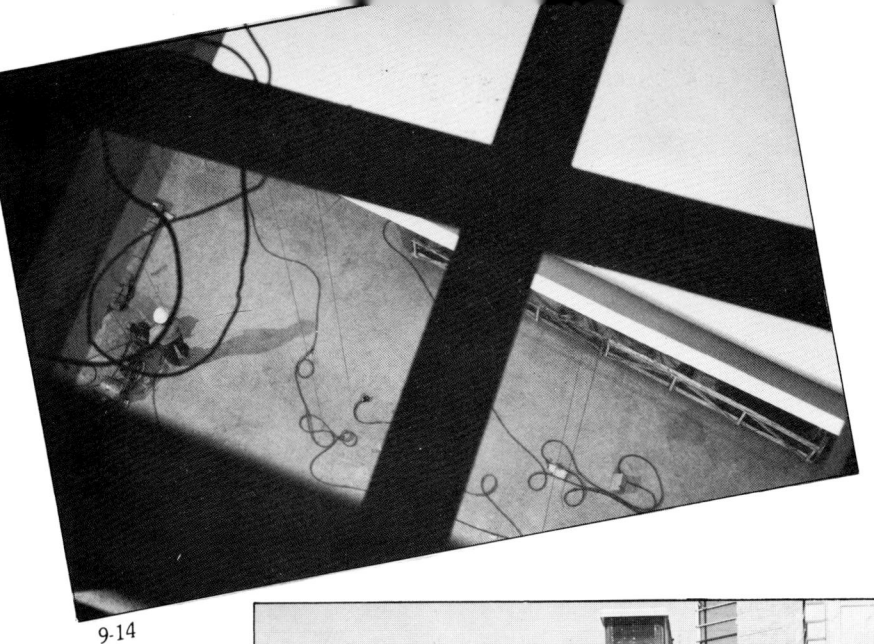

9-14

9-15

OUR NEW FACILITY

9-14 *View through upper ceiling access port, April 1985*

9-15 *Entrance canopy, April 1985*

tive stage of construction, was that it was going to be a very exciting project.

"Perhaps as a result of the controversy and the years that were involved in the project, I was also very impressed that it was very well thought out and thoroughly done at that point."

The concept had changed considerably during those 14 years of delay. It had begun as a full-blown complex, very much a pipe dream, and gradually evolved into the more affordable single performance space. Not what was originally wanted, to be sure, nor what might have been afforded at the time had all things fallen into place when they should have, but an excellent facility nonetheless. It seats 1,550 people, and the architects have done their best to bring audience and performers as close together as possible.

The facility can easily be adapted to a full house symphony concert, rock opera, dramatic production, or the quiet intimacy of a folk singer. This can be done through four moveable elements around the stage: the canopy, the sound bridge, and the two hydraulic orchestra lifts. Acoustics are state-of-the-art, as are sight lines. The seats are comfortable, and the place is air conditioned.

The building is fully accessible and barrier free. The acoustics and support systems make it ideal for television production should the need arise. It can also accommodate the making of sound recordings.

In comparison with other cities, Thunder Bay's $14.5 million price tag was a bargain. Kitchener paid more than that, as did Hamilton, while Calgary's new complex, which opened just a month before ours did, cost $80 million, with a theatre portion worth $38 million and offering only 300 more seats than ours.

"They paid a lot more per foot than we did," says Clint Kuschak, "and they're getting basically the same thing performance-wise as we have. Also, we'll probably be seen to have got a lot of bargains dollar-wise, when the international media see what we have. That will probably allow other North American centres to take another look at ways of getting a good performance facility in their communities at reasonably low dollars."

The total operating costs of our new Auditorium are estimated at $1.7 million per year, partially offset by an annual City grant of $400,000. The latter, aimed at keeping ticket prices affordable, amounts to

9-16

9-16 *Concert ceilings installed, April 1985*

9-17 *Scaffolding goes up to facilitate work on the upper ceiling, May 1985*

9-17

9-18

approximately three dollars per year per person, but in the long run, our local economy should experience a definite growth that could make that cost very worthwhile.

According to Auditorium staff, studies have shown that Broadway means millions of dollars per year to New York City's businesses. In Duluth, an extensive survey of the Arena/Auditorium complex has shown that for every dollar spent on the operations, the community receives ten in return through its stores, malls, hotels and related facilities. We too will derive similar benefits.

"We felt that ten-to-one might be high when we were making our case to the OMB," says Clint Kuschak. "So we opted for a benefit factor of five-to-one. Based on an operating budget of $900,000, we should get back over $4 million. If you add in the City's annual grant, then it's closer to six."

And as a result of our newest addition to Canadian entertainment, there is now a chain of modern performance facilities from coast to coast, which should contribute to some truly fascinating concert tours.

So who will buy all the tickets?

We will, mostly. But our visitors will buy them, too. They've been coming here in gradually increasing numbers for many decades, because of the attractions we've been accumulating. Our ski resorts now draw thousands of spectators for world events every winter, and ski tours as well. We see hundreds of excursions pass through here every summer. Many of them pull into our hotels and motels to spend the night, and when such things are planned ahead of time -- as they usually are -- there'll be time allotted for the enjoyment of local entertainment. After all, people from Thunder Bay take the same kind of trips to other places, to do the same things.

Residents of Thunder Bay are nevertheless concerned about the possibilities of their new Auditorium standing idle much of the time, despite the ambitious seasons that have been announced. Therefore, many are inclined to ask how often must this facility be used to break even financially?

"We're looking at doing around 125 performances and another 40 rehearsals," says Mr. McCurdy. "That's the break-even point in our initial year. We hope to get that up to somewhere around 175 to 200 per-

9-19

... We're in the business to promote the arts in Northwestern Ontario ...

9-18 Rigging for battens above grid level of the fly area, May 1985

9-19 Concert ceilings in storage position within the fly area, May 1985

formances in about three years' time. Initial responses make it look like our original estimate will be exceeded, because, by the end of July, 1985, we already had 90 commitments, and we were still months away from opening."

At that time, the Auditorium was in the midst of a very vigorous campaign to sell season tickets, and it looked to many as though their plan was to sell out every seat in the house ahead of time, for every show. In which case, what about the tourists?

"We're holding open seats for every company that comes in," says Mr. McCurdy, "so there will always be seats available, although they could be fairly limited in number."

And what will the average ticket prices be?

"Our normal prices for the majority of events," he says, "are in a three-price range: $12, $14, and $16. A couple of these, such as the Gala opening, were more. The special evening with Bob Hope, was $50 per seat, and there will be a few in the $18 to $22 range. But the majority will fall in the $12 to $16 area, and there'll even be a few as low as four or five dollars."

But it was obvious to many, as the Auditorium began to rise, that some local groups might never use it. The theatre companies, for instance; small instrumental ensembles, even larger choirs. And since it had been our local performing artists who, in having achieved their own levels of excellence, had helped local audiences evolve to the point where an auditorium was realistically viable, would they not suffer because of the same facility they had helped bring about?

Mr. McCurdy is optimistic:

"We're looking at what our role is in this community," he says. "We've really seen it as an industry-wide role, and we don't see ourselves as just being in the business of promoting the Community Auditorium. We're in the business to promote the arts in Thunder Bay, and really in Northwestern Ontario. We feel that because of our size and impact on the community, and our visibility in the community, that we can give the arts a much higher profile.

"I think, then, it's up to us to help the arts groups in Thunder Bay to take advantage of that. But we've created, I think, a whole new audience out there. It really provides an opportunity for the other groups

151

to take advantage of that.

"Basically, what we're talking about is the 'entertainment pie', and that's going to grow, so everybody's piece will get bigger. A lot of people see the 'pie' remaining the same size, and now, all of a sudden, we're going to come in and take three quarters of it. That outlook isn't unique to Thunder Bay, because it has happened in every community that has ever built a facility like this. But the effect that these communities have found is that, in effect, the existing pie is really just one quarter to one third of the potential pie that could exist.

"Take Lethbridge, for instance; the place I just came from. The city had a facility themselves, so when the University built a four-theatre complex, community organizations were terrified that the city facility would close down. They saw the 'pie' remaining the same, and this new facility having to run 200 performances a year, and all.

"Well, what happened was that the city facility filled their dates, as did the university, so the community more than doubled the amount of entertainment available. And everybody was selling out. It created a tremendous new audience. The symphony went from a deficit situation to actually turning a profit."

"Things are obviously much more competitve, but I think people respond to that competitiveness and upgrade, and everybody benefits. That definitely happened in Lethbridge. The same sort of problems existed there in the first year and a half that are in evidence here, but after four years, people began to realize that a tremendous growth had taken place, and the community was really enriched by what was going on.

"So our goal is to expand that pie and give the other arts groups access to our audiences, and try to help them grow. And that's whether they actually perform in this auditorium or have their own distinctive locations."

In terms of actual use of the Auditorium, Mr. McCurdy feels that some groups can combine efforts and take better advantage of the facility. Also, he and his staff are quite prepared to work with local groups to help them lessen their financial responsibilities, by having the Auditorium itself assume some of the risk. All such cases will be looked at individually, and what

9-20 Acoustic canopy at its lowest position shows framework construction, June 1985

9-21 Maple hardwood flooring is laid stage area, July 1985

9-22 Workmen installing dias in lower lobby, July 1985

9-23 Lighting is completed in the loge and balcony areas, July 1985

9-20

9-21

9-22

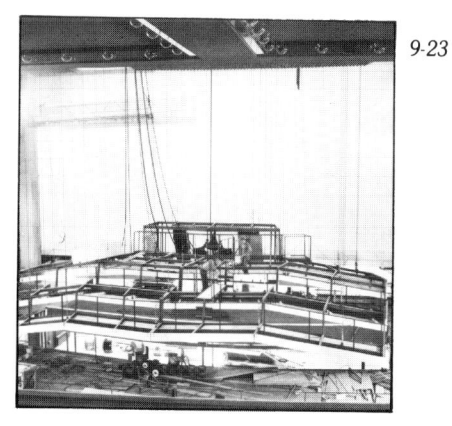

9-23

can be done will be done, he says.

"We realized when we got into this, that it was a major transition financially for a lot of local groups to use the facility," he says. "Obviously their expenses will be a lot higher than, say, at the University or Selkirk. However, their potential revenue is also much greater. Moreover, we have a professional staff here, and part of their mandate is to work with community groups. The Public Relations Department, for instance, will help them sell the event, or give them advice on how to generate the most revenue. Obviously, we can't give them free advertising, but the expertise is here and available to anybody who wants it. And we feel that in the first couple of years, we have to get these people in here, let them try our facility, and realize the potential revenue that is out there."

He was also quick to add that there is nothing, from the Auditorium's point of view, to stop a local group from sponsoring outside talent. Even, for instance, one of the choirs bringing in a top performer and being part of the show, themselves.

"I guess the closest parallel with us and the community," says Mr. McCurdy, "would be the local ski industry. From what I've heard since I arrived, each little ski place used to think of itself as competing with all the others. And then, suddenly, they all looked at the whole picture, and realized that the ski industry was an entity in itself, and that if they all banded together, they would attract people in greater numbers, and all of them would benefit accordingly. It can be like that, too, in the performing arts."

To that end, the Thunder Bay Regional Arts Council is alive and well. If anything, it's stronger now than it was back in the days of the Lakehead School of Fine Arts, so the arts forum is ready and waiting.

And so the dream which began away back in the Depression has finally materialized. It isn't the facility that was envisioned on the 'wish list', but that doesn't make it less worthy of the community that finally built it. The visual arts will rarely use it, but after all, they have the National Exhibition Centre and Centre for Indian Art, which is already operating. Other organizations, such as the Thunder Bay Symphony Orchestra, certainly will use our Auditorium, as will some of the choirs, but the farther down the list you go, the more you'll find that won't.

153

9-24 *Landscaping starts around the auditorium's exterior, August 1985*

9-25 *Minister of Northern Affairs, Leo Bernier enlists the aid of MPP Mickey Hennessy in presenting a cheque in the amount of $250,000 to Dr. Charles Johnston*

9-26 *The seats are readied for installation. Brian McCurdy looks on. August, 1985*

9-24

When that happens, it doesn't necessarily mean that the Auditorium has failed in its purpose, but rather that performances are continuing to be staged in the facilities most suited to the occasion. The Auditorium is still an excellent venue which should easily prove itself to have been well worth the effort.

Or, as its first Chairman, Dan O'Gorman says:

"It is definitely a milestone for Thunder Bay's performing arts. One which will provide a quality of life in the city that has not been here. It will be an appropriate place to go and view; and an appropriate place for our different organizations to use and in which to produce quality entertainment, and in which to grow and develop further."

On this final page on the 39th day, the temptation is strong to pontificate; to champion excellence, make predictions, rehash with emphasis. But it wasn't intended to be a complete story in the first place; merely a general panorama, as it were, of a truly fantastic saga of ordinary people doing the things they enjoy doing.

Therefore, let me borrow from television, and merely toss you some slides of things you've already encountered herein. They're four direct quotations from the interviews that went into this project. Think about them, and then, if you wish, try to guess who said them.

****

"This Auditorium will certainly change our cultural life dramatically. Nobody knows its real impact yet, but things are going to change, and change very fast."

****

"The entertainment pie is going to grow, so everybody's piece will get bigger."

****

"I just hope that when these performers finish their sets, that the people will applaud them."

****

"You're only as good as your next opening night. It doesn't matter what you've done in the past, the only thing that counts is your next performance."

****

9-25

9-26

9-27

9-27 *Thunder Bay's Auditorium was designed by a consortium of City architects*

The Opening

The Opening

BOARD OF DIRECTORS
Thunder Bay Community Auditorium Inc.

Allan Laakkonen
VICE-PRESIDENT

James Rapino
TREASURER

Darlene Chuchmuch Kohanski
SECRETARY

Ken Boshcoff
Pat Gamble
Florence Johnston
Taras Kozyra
W. Sterling Lysnes
Jack Mallon
Ross Mitchell
Reeve Peter Romanuk
Doug W. Scott
Lawrence Timko
Dick Waddington
Dale Willoughby

Hubert Badanai, Sr.
HONORARY CHAIRMAN

James A. Martin
HONORARY SECRETARY

PAST PRESIDENTS
Dan O'Gorman
Bob Boorman
David Hurdon
Gary Polonsky
Anthonie V. Wooldridge
Charles M. Johnston, M.D.

10-1   *Exterior Graphic*

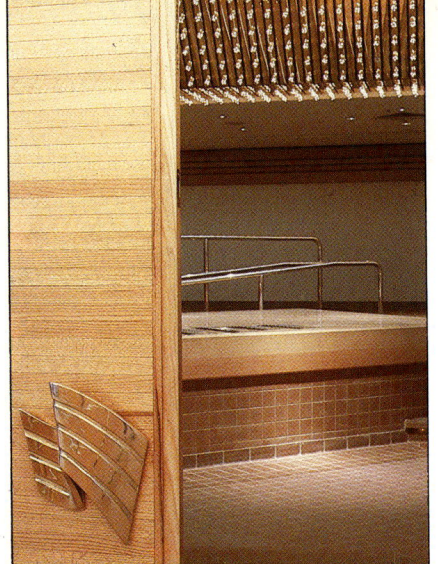

The Board of Directors of the Thunder Bay Community Auditorium Inc. extend our great appreciation for the continued support and generosity of those firms who became "Performance" Sponsors. Your significant assistance has brought us all closer to completing our dream.

SPONSORSHIP PLEDGES:

Advertising Agencies:

Henderson and Associates Marketing and Advertising Ltd.
272 Park Avenue   345-3255

Mallon's - The Advertising Agency
1184 Roland Street   622-9661

Airline:

Air Canada
Thunder Bay Airport   623-3313

Chiropractic:

Thomas G. Jessiman D.C.
2813 East Arthur Street   623-6500

Computer Systems - Business:

Entre Computer Centre
406 Memorial Avenue   345-2919

Donut Shops:

Northco Foods Limited
1046 Memorial Avenue   623-4453

Financial Planning:

Capital Financial Services
Ste. 300, 28 N. Cumberland Street   345-1485

Furniture Retailing:

The Final Touch
125 S. Vickers Street   623-2523

Hair Stylist:

Current River Beauty Salon
387 Cuyler Street   683-8661

Hotel:

Airlane Motor Hotel
698 Arthur Street West   577-1181

10-2   A discriminating eye is all that is needed to complete the finishing details on our Auditorium's lobby

10-3   Backstage, acoustic and lighting systems are discussed and made functional

10-4   An unpretentious, elegant interior awaits city audiences

10-5   The polished and refined styling of the Auditorium's front entrance beckons patrons of the performing arts

10-6   Chip, the Thunder Bay Community Auditorium's mascot, leads a parade to Canada's newest performing arts centre

10-7   The German Folksingers directed by Wally Kesmarky are one of several multicultural groups entertaining audiences during the facility's opening week

10-6

10-7

10-8

10-9

10-10

10-11

10-12

10-13

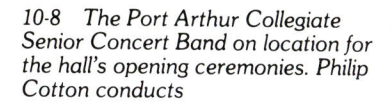

10-8 The Port Arthur Collegiate Senior Concert Band on location for the hall's opening ceremonies. Philip Cotton conducts

10-9 We've done it, Thunder Bay! Our place to applaud has been realized. Participating in the Ribbon Cutting Ceremony are (left to right) Acting Mayor Joe Climenhage, Parliamentary Assistant Remo Mancini MPP, Chairperson of the Canada Council Maureen Forrester, Vice-President of the Auditorium's Board of Directors Allan Laakkonen and Board of Directors' Representative Florence Johnston

10-10 Ontario Minister of Citizenship and Culture, Lily Munro announces a supplementary grant of $500,000. at the opening dinner

10-11 Opening night audience

10-12 The affable Peter Gzowski is master of ceremonies

10-13 Ballet sensation, Karen Kain is the first to dance on the country's newest stage

10-14 Kevin Pugh and Yoko Ichino perform the final pas de deux from "Don Quixote"

10-15 The Canadian Brass entertain and amuse the audience

10-16 Mezzanine lobby during intermission

10-17 Maureen Forrester performs "Handel avia Per Rendermi Beato"

10-17

10-16

10-14

10-15

161

10-18 Master showman, Bob Hope delights a fullhouse

10-19 Dinah Christie meets with city arts patrons

10-20 Bob and Dolores Hope backstage after their performances

Office Equip. and Supplies:

Lowerys Ltd.
581 Red River Road   344-6666

Pharmacy:

Gascoigne's Drug Store
115 W. Arthur Street   577-1131

Printing:

Lakehead Printing
1184 Roland Street   623-4652

SRC Shel/Don Reproduction Centre Ltd.
Ste. 107, 1265 E. Arthur Street   623-1371

Restaurant:

Casey's Restaurants
450 Memorial Avenue   345-4562

PHOTO ACKNOWLEDGEMENTS

0-1 Courtesy Thunder Bay Community Auditorium
0-2 Thunder Bay Historical Museum Society (T.B.H.M.S.) 979.73.13
0-3 T.B.H.M.S. 984.1.799
0-4 Courtesy Barbara Heerema
0-5 T.B.H.M.S. 973.3.182

1-1 Courtesy Sylvia Horn
1-2 T.B.H.M.S. 973.28.15B
1-3 T.B.H.M.S. 975.113.316
1-4 T.B.H.M.S. 975.1.510
1-5 T.B.H.M.S. 978.126.4
1-6 Courtesy Brodie Resource Library P563
1-7 T.B.H.M.S. 978.126.2
1-8 T.B.H.M.S. 978.11.76
1-9 Courtesy Brodie Resource Library P689
1-10 T.B.H.M.S. 975-1.423
1-11 T.B.H.M.S. 973.110.15
1-12 T.B.H.M.S. 972.15.3

2-1 T.B.H.M.S. 972-2.371
2-2 T.B.H.M.S. 972-110-38
2-3 Courtesy Ida Colosimo
2-4 Courtesy Ida Colosimo
2-5 Courtesy Ida Colosimo
2-6 Courtesy Jean Crittall
2-7 Courtesy Jean Crittal

3-1 Courtesy Fort William Male Choir Archives
3-2 Courtesy Fort William Male Choir Archives
3-3 Courtesy Fort William Male Choir Archives
3-4 Courtesy Fort William Male Choir Archives
3-5 T.B.H.M.S. 978.13.59
3-6 Courtesy Lakehead Choral Group Archives
3-7 Courtesy Lakehead Choral Group Archives
3-8 T.B.H.M.S. 984.80.103B
3-9 Courtesy Lakehead Choral Group Archives
3-10 Courtesy Thunder Bay Barbershop Chorus Archives
3-11 Courtesy Sweet Adelines Archives
3-12 Courtesy Betty Karpiuk
3-13 T.B.H.M.S. 975.83.24
3-14 T.B.H.M.S. 972.64.42
3-15 T.B.H.M.S. 981.71.3

4-1 T.B.H.M.S. 973.28.15C
4-2 Courtesy Sylvia Horn
4-3 Courtesy Multicultural Association of Northwestern Ontario Archives
4-4 Courtesy Amelia Jackson
4-5 T.B.H.M.S. 984.80.124C
4-6 Courtesy Multicultural Association of Northwestern Ontario Archives
4-7 Courtesy Lyons Dance Troupe
4-8 Courtesy Lyons Dance Troupe
4-9 Courtesy Thunder Bay Community Auditorium
4-10 Courtesy Sylvia Horn
4-11 Courtesy Amelia Jackson
4-12 Courtesy Sylvia Horn
4-13 Courtesy Sylvia Horn

5-1 T.B.H.M.S. 983.18.3
5-2 Courtesy Brodie Resource Library
5-3 T.B.H.M.S. 984.53.30F
5-4 T.B.H.M.S. 984.53.30G
5-5 T.B.H.M.S. 984.53.30E
5-6 Courtesy Chancellor Paterson Library L.U. MG3 XIII 54
5-7 Courtesy Chancellor Paterson Library L.U. D3203 Archive 224e
5-8 Courtesy Chancellor Paterson Library L.U. MG3 XIII
5-9 Courtesy Chancellor Paterson Library L.U. Archive 193a
5-10 T.B.H.M.S. 972-110.7b
5-11 T.B.H.M.S. 972.110.7b
5-12 T.B.H.M.S. 972.110.7b
5-13 Courtesy Brodie Resource Library
5-14 T.B.H.M.S. 984.53.1A
5-15 T.B.H.M.S. 984.53.1B
5-16 T.B.H.M.S. 973.28.15A
5-17 Courtesy Lorne Delinsky
5-18 Courtesy Moonlight Melodrama Archives
5-19 Courtesy Moonlight Melodrama Archives
5-20 Courtesy Moonlight Melodrama Archives
5-21 Courtesy Magnus Theatre Archives
5-22 Courtesy Magnus Theatre Archives
5-23 Courtesy Magnus Theatre Archives
5-24 Courtesy Magnus Theatre Archives
5-25 Courtesy Magnus Theatre Archives
5-26 Courtesy Kam Theatre Archives
5-27 Courtesy Kam Theatre Archives
5-28 Courtesy Kam Theatre Archives
5-29 T.B.H.M.S. 973.150.1
5-30 T.B.H.M.S. 973.150.1
5-31 T.B.H.M.S. 973.150.1
5-32 T.B.H.M.S. 973.150.1

6-1 Courtesy Ida Colosimo
6-2 Courtesy Helen Anderson
6-3 T.B.H.M.S. 975.1.55
6-4 T.B.H.M.S. 983.59.2 (JJJJJ)
6-5 Courtesy Thunder Bay Community Auditorium
6-6 Vivid Photos
6-7 T.B.H.M.S. 975.1.49
6-8 Courtesy Bob Balabuk
6-9 Vivid Photos
6-10 Courtesy Betty Karpiuk

7-1 Courtesy Shirley Shaffer
7-2 Courtesy Shirley Shaffer
7-3 Courtesy Bruce Anderson
7-4 Courtesy Shirley Shaffer
7-5 Courtesy Tom Horricks
7-6 Vivid Photos
7-7 Vivid Photos
7-8 Courtesy Tom Horricks

8-1 Courtesy Jennifer Rhine
8-2 Vivid Photos
8-3 Courtesy Thunder Bay Community Auditorium
8-4 Courtesy Jean Crittall
8-5 T.B.H.M.S. Hean Crittal Collection Box 2
8-6 Courtesy Jennifer Rhine
8-7 Courtesy Jennifer Rhine
8-8 Courtesy Jennifer Rhine
8-9 Courtesy Thunder Bay Community Auditorium
8-10 Vivid Photos
8-11 Vivid Photos

9-1 to 9-27   Vivid Photos

10-1 to 10-20   Vivid Photos

ABOUT THE AUTHOR

George Campbell is one of Northwestern Ontario's most prolific freelance writers currently practising in Thunder Bay. As such, he serves a wide variety of clients, for whom he produces an equally varied range of material. As a result, he has written speeches, radio ads, television commercials, pamphlets, promotional pieces, circular letters, newspaper supplements, news releases, brochures, dedications, audio-visual scripts, and even books.

In the latter category, Mr. Campbell did his first in 1980, and **Performance** is his ninth. He has also written two novels.

At one time or another, Mr. Campbell has contributed to such major Canadian publications as *Manitoba Business, The Financial Post,* and *The Globe and Mail.* He has been heard on national radio and his material has been read on the networks by others. He was, until recently, Regional Editor for the magazine *Trade and Commerce,* and a feature writer for *Northern Ontario Business.* He has accepted assignments from *Lake Superior Port Cities,* in Duluth, and *Northern Ontario Sportsman* in Sault Ste. Marie.

Locally, George has been read in such publications as *Chamber Chat, Lakehead Living, Thunder Bay Guest, Thunder Bay Guide (T.V. Listings),* and has occasionally contributed to *Today in the City,* and others. On radio, he has contributed commentaries to CBQ's *Daybreak* and *The Great Northwest,* and was the original host of CHFD-FM's *ARTS 94.*

George Campbell was born in Kelliher, Saskatchewan, in 1926. He received his elementary schooling in Brandon, Manitoba, and then became a landline commercial morse operator with Canadian Pacific Telegraphs. Having married and begun to raise a family, he returned to high school in Dryden in 1954, and acquired university degrees from Manitoba and Lakehead Universities.

He taught chemistry from 1962 until 1975, and is now an elementary school librarian in Thunder Bay.